SECURING OUR FUTURE

Embracing the Resilience and Brilliance of Black Women in Cyber.

BY:

TALYA PARKER, DR. MONA LISA PINKNEY, DEIDRA PHYALL,
TANNEASHA GORDON, MARI GALLOWAY, CARLA PLUMMER,
TIA HOPKINS, TENNISHA MARTIN, SHINESA CAMBRIC, ZINET KEMAL,
DR. DIANA B. ALLEN, TASHYA DENOSE, JULIET OKAFOR,
JARELL OSHODI, COURTNEY H. JACKSON, & CAMILLE STEWART GLOSTER

Published by Live Limitless Media Group LLC
Publishing@sierrarainge.com
info@livelimitlessmedia.com

The Black Women in Cyber Collective
Contact Information:
Email: info@blkwicc.com
Website: www.blkwicc.com

Printed in the United States of America

ISBN: 978-1-952-903-45-8

Dedication

To the resilient women of color who break barriers, shatter glass ceilings, and light the path for the generations that follow.

For the girl who keeps second-guessing her greatness while navigating the feelings of an imposter. For the girl who is tired of navigating microaggressions and gaslighting. For the girl who comes from a 1st generation American family, and has to carry the burden of lifting the ones before you and those to come after you. For the girl who feels like giving up.

You belong.

Your time is now.

Yes, you absolutely can.

You are smart enough.

You are strong enough.

You are deserving.

This book is dedicated to the trailblazers, the innovators, the disruptors, and the warriors who have defied stereotypes, overcome obstacles, and redefined the landscape of cyber. Your unwavering determination, unyielding strength, and unbreakable spirit inspire us all.

May your stories be heard, your voices amplified, and your contributions celebrated. You have not only secured networks and data but have also fortified the walls of possibility for countless others. Your presence in the cyber field enriches it with diverse perspectives and a wealth of talents, making it stronger, more inclusive, and more resilient.

As we continue to forge ahead, let this book serve as a testament to your excellence and a source of inspiration for women of color aspiring to make their mark in this vital and dynamic industry. Together, we rise, empower, and lead the way to a brighter, safer, and more equitable digital future.

With profound admiration and gratitude,

- Talya C. Parker

Acknowledgment

When I first conceived the idea for this collective, it seemed like a distant dream. But as the cyber visionary I've grown to become, I recognized the pressing need for what we set out to accomplish in our space. I want to express my profound gratitude to these incredible women who joined me on this amazing journey, sharing their stories, embracing vulnerability, and uplifting those who will follow in our footsteps:

Tashya Denose, my brilliant, beautiful, creative friend turned sister, and I have poured countless sleepless nights and tireless days into this labor of love. Tashya has been my right hand in so many areas of my life, both personal and professional. Thank you, Tashya, for all that you continue to do. She stands out as a transformative figure in the cybersecurity sector, not just as a professional but also as a passionate advocate with a mission to empower women and redefine the field through emotional intelligence. With extensive experience spanning various roles in the US Department of Defense, US Secret Service, Intelligence community, and corporations like Google and Meta's Reality Labs, Tashya fervently works towards uplifting black women in cyber and privacy roles, hosting the thoughtful podcast "Do We Belong Here," and emphasizing the essential roles of empathy and emotional intelligence in the industry often defined solely by technology.

Mona Lisa Pinkney, my amazing mentor, has been my unwavering support system, lifting me in countless ways for which I'll forever be indebted. Mona Lisa's accomplishments are nothing short of astounding. She is a renowned Global and Local Keynote speaker, celebrated not only for her brilliance but also for her profound impact. Her recognition as one of the Top 30 Most Admired Minority Professionals in Cybersecurity by SeQure World Magazine is a testament to her influence and expertise. In addition to these accolades, Mona Lisa stands as the proud recipient of the 2019 Maryland Innovation & Security Institute's (MISI) Contemporary Woman in STEM award, an honor that underscores her dedication and innovation in the field. Furthermore, her acknowledgment as a Woman to Watch in Cybersecurity by Forbes Magazine serves as a testament to her trailblazing career. Mona Lisa, your unwavering support, guidance, and the example you've set have shaped my journey in immeasurable ways. I am eternally grateful for your presence and mentorship in my life.

Tia Hopkins, my friend and mentor, is an absolute force of nature and has spent over two decades in the IT Security industry. Our initial encounter was during a virtual fireside chat, where I was immediately captivated by her unapologetic demeanor, brilliance, and warm energy. Following that chat, I reached out to Tia in the virtual realm, and our connection deepened as we celebrated each other's achievements and exchanged valuable guidance. Notably, Tia also runs a non-profit organization, further strengthening our bond. Our first in-person meeting took place at the Black Women in STEM Summit, an encounter that solidified our connection. Tia currently holds the esteemed position of Chief Cyber Resilience Officer & Field CTO at eSentire, and she is the driving force behind Empow(H)er Cybersecurity, a non-profit organization dedicated to inspiring and empowering women of color in the cybersecurity field. Tia, your unwavering support and willingness to embark on this co-authorship journey with me means the world. Your confidence and presence are deeply appreciated, and I am profoundly grateful for our enduring connection.

Carla Plummer holds a special place in my heart as a childhood friend. Our journey together dates back to our days at Sunrise Middle, and I'm genuinely thrilled to have her as a vital part of this venture. Her contributions to the industry have been nothing short of remarkable, and she has played a significant role in my personal growth as a leader of BGiC. Carla possesses a unique quality: she may not speak often, but when she does, her words carry weight and wisdom. With over 12 years of experience in IT and Information Security, she has carved an impressive path as an accomplished engineer. Beyond her professional achievements, Carla's unwavering commitment as a wife, mother, and versatile Cyber Professional is truly commendable.

Camille Stewart Gloster, Esq, I met Camille at a Women in Cybersecurity panel during the RSA conference, and as I sat next to her, I was immediately struck by her incredible presence. Following the conference, our connection continued to flourish in the virtual realm. When an opportunity arose for me at Google, I wasted no time in securing a spot on Camille's busy calendar. What began as occasional meetings soon evolved into a profound mentorship that blossomed into a deep and cherished friendship. Camille possesses a unique gift – she is the kind of person who effortlessly elevates those around her. She is a genuine advocate for inclusivity, consistently seeking opportunities to give back and share the stage. Camille's brilliance and unwavering drive have propelled her to shatter numerous glass ceilings in her remarkable career. However, what resonates with me most about my friend is her unyielding belief that "there is room for you, too." This philosophy is not just a sentiment but a principle she embodies in every aspect of her life. I count myself incredibly fortunate to have shared space and time with this exceptional human being. Camille Stewart Gloster, Esq., currently serving as the Deputy National Cyber Director for Technology and Ecosystem at the White House, is a globally recognized expert in the fields of cyber, technology, and national security strategy and policy. Her career has left an indelible mark across the private, public, and non-profit sectors, and her impact continues to inspire all who have the privilege of knowing her.

Courtney H. Jackson has always been someone I admired from a distance, when Tia suggested I reach out to her, I eagerly seized the opportunity. Courtney's entrepreneurial journey in this field is nothing short of commendable and represents a path that many of us aspire to but often hesitate to pursue due to fear. Her story is a powerful narrative that can liberate those of us who seek higher ceilings and greater depth in navigating this space. Courtney is not just a notable figure; she's a multi-award-winning Founder and CEO of Paragon Cyber Solutions, LLC. Her impressive accolades include being named the 2023 Tampa Bay Business Journal BusinessWoman of the Year Honoree and the 2022 Global Cybersecurity Woman Entrepreneur of the Year. Furthermore, she plays a pivotal role as the Vice President of Women in Defense Greater Tampa Bay.

Deidra Phyall I would like to extend my heartfelt gratitude to Deidra Phyall, a remarkable individual whose unwavering support has been a beacon of strength throughout my journey into motherhood. Deidra constantly leaves me in awe with her unyielding commitment to our shared mission and her genuine servant's heart. Deidra, a proud native of North Carolina, epitomizes the essence of devotion as a loving mother, an advocate for Historically Black Colleges and Universities (HBCUs), and a dedicated board member of BGiC. Her remarkable contributions also extend into the realm of cyber education and workforce development, where she has made a lasting impact. Deidra's impressive list of accolades, including the Leading Change Award in Diversity, Equity, and Inclusion from Women Who Code, the prestigious SANS Difference Maker Mentor of the Year Award, and recognition as one of the 21 Women in Cybersecurity and 1 Million Women in STEM, speaks volumes about her exceptional achievements in these fields. Deidra Phyall's profound influence and dedication have been instrumental in shaping my path, and for that, I am profoundly grateful. Her accomplishments serve as an inspiration to us all, and I am honored to have her on this co-authorship journey as a peer-mentor and friend.

Diana B. Allen. I would like to extend my deepest gratitude to Diana, a trusted colleague and dear friend whose impact on my life and the success of BGiC (Black Girls in Cybersecurity) cannot be overstated. Our paths first crossed many moons ago when we were both colleagues at one of the world's top Big 4 consulting firms. It was there that Diana selflessly guided me through the intricacies of the consulting world, imparting invaluable wisdom and knowledge that continue to shape my journey. Diana, your willingness to wholeheartedly embark on this journey with me has been a source of immeasurable strength and inspiration. Diana is a globally recognized speaker celebrated for her profound insights into leadership and technology. Her distinguished doctorate in organizational leadership attests to her dedication and commitment to pioneering research, with a special focus on "Empowerment & the Career Sponsorship of Women in STEM." Diana, your enduring support, mentorship, and outstanding achievements have left an indelible mark on my life. I am deeply thankful to have you by my side, and I look forward to the continued journey ahead with you as an ever-present guiding force.

Jarell Oshodi, a true New Orleans native, devoted mother, accomplished data privacy attorney, dedicated career federal servant, captivating keynote speaker, and corporate trainer. As a valued board member of Black Girls in Cyber, she has brought her unique blend of talents to our shared mission. My introduction to Jarell was a serendipitous encounter through her Instagram account. Upon discovering that she held the distinguished position of Deputy Chief Privacy Officer and was the mastermind behind privacy trainings, I knew that I needed to enlist this beacon of "Black Girl Magic" onto our team. Jarell's remarkable qualities, from her humor and friendship to her thoughtfulness, have grown to occupy a special place in my heart. She is more than a friend; she's like a sister – a source of unwavering support and unfiltered honesty. When I approached Jarell with the proposition of co-authoring this book, she surprised me by already having her chapter ready. It was as if fate had predetermined her role as the perfect addition to our endeavor. Jarell, I extend my heartfelt thanks for your trust, belief in the vision, and for embarking on this co-authorship journey with me. Your presence elevates this project, and I am grateful for your unwavering support.

Juliet Okafor, JD or "Jules" as she's affectionately known, is a true powerhouse in the realms of law, cybersecurity, and gender equality. Her unwavering passion for justice, profound commitment to family, and dedication to advancing women in the cybersecurity field have positioned her as a leading figure in Security Culture, Privacy, and DevSecOps. I had the privilege of crossing paths with Jules during an RSA Women In Cybersecurity event. As a fellow panelist, I couldn't help but be captivated by her vibrant and commanding presence. Her thought-provoking and enriching perspectives had the entire room hanging on her every word, leaving me wondering why she wasn't up on that panel with us from the start. Our connection from that day forward has remained strong, and when I extended an invitation to Jules to join this journey, her immediate and enthusiastic "yes" was a testament to her unwavering support. Jules, I am deeply grateful for your faith in the vision and your willingness to join this endeavor. Your presence and expertise are invaluable, and I thank you from the bottom of my heart for being an integral part of this project.

Mari Galloway, a true luminary in the world of cybersecurity and a shining example of excellence. Her impressive accolades as a multi-award-winning cyber professional, published author, captivating keynote speaker, LinkedIn Learning instructor, and the CEO of Cyberjutsu, a national nonprofit dedicated to empowering women and girls in cybersecurity, are a testament to her remarkable achievements. From afar, I've always held Mari in high regard, especially the way she leads Cyberjutsu. I've had the privilege of witnessing her talks, where her confidence and vibrant personality shine through, leaving a lasting impression. It was always a hope that our paths would cross and I would get to know her better. When I first conceived the idea for this project and shared it with Tia, she highly recommended Mari, and my excitement knew no bounds. Deep down, I had hoped Mari would be a part of this journey. Since embarking on this venture, I've been fortunate enough to not only meet Mari but also experience her humble and kind spirit up close. I eagerly anticipate building a deeper sisterhood through our collaboration. Mari, I extend my heartfelt gratitude to you for joining me on this incredible journey. Your expertise and presence enrich this project, and I am honored to have you as a cherished partner in this endeavor.

Shinesa Cambric, a devoted mother of three teens, a distinguished board member, a trusted startup advisor, a best-selling author, and an award-winning cyber innovator with two patents pending, embodies the essence of excellence. In her role as a technology leader at Microsoft and as an instructor with O'Reilly, she extends her expertise to contribute to certifications by esteemed organizations like CompTIA, CertNexus, and the Cloud Security Alliance. My introduction to Shinesa occurred through LinkedIn in November 2020, thanks to the gracious connection made by my beautiful friend (may God rest her soul), Theo GrayMccarty. Shinesa was actively involved in promoting

Black women in cybersecurity, and Theo believed that I should be part of this distinguished group. Since that serendipitous introduction, I have been consistently awestruck by Shinesa and her remarkable accomplishments in this field. She exudes humility and kindness, and possesses an unwavering spirit that makes her a total badass in her own right. I consider it an immense blessing to have the opportunity to co-author alongside Shinesa. She serves as a guiding light for those who will follow in her footsteps, and her impact on this journey is immeasurable. Thank you, sis, for sharing your wisdom and joining me in this co-authorship endeavor. Your presence enriches this project, and I am honored to stand alongside you as we inspire others in the realm of cybersecurity.

Tanneasha Gordon, also affectionately known as the Olivia Pope of Privacy and Content Compliance, is a brilliant executive and inspiring friend whose steadfast support has been instrumental in this project and my leadership of Black Girls in Cyber. She is a National Association of Female Executives (NAFE) a Woman of Excellence award recipient, a sought-after speaker, and sits on several boards including Black Girls in Cyber. Her presence in my journey and her contributions to the world of cybersecurity and female empowerment are immeasurable. Tanneasha, I am deeply grateful for your support and friendship. You have played an indispensable role in this endeavor and my leadership at BGiC. Thank you for being the exceptional person you are.

Tennisha Martin has been the North Star guiding my path as the Founder of Black Girls in Cyber. In the midst of managing her own insanely successful foundation, BlackGirlsHack. Tennisha selflessly offered her invaluable insights, providing me with a compass to navigate the complexities of running a non-profit organization. Tennisha wears many hats with grace and distinction. She is a devoted wife, a captivating speaker, an accomplished author and educator, a sought-after instructor on LinkedIn Learning, and an award-winning hacker. Above all, she is the visionary founder of BlackGirlsHack, an international non-profit organization that stands as a beacon for increasing diversity and inclusion within the field of cybersecurity. Tennisha's impact on my journey and her monumental contributions to the realm of cybersecurity and diversity are immeasurable. Her dedication and wisdom have been a guiding force, and I am profoundly grateful for her presence in my life and in the mission of Black Girls in Cyber.

Zinet Kemal, a resilient immigrant mother of four, is a remarkable force to be reckoned with. Her list of accolades is nothing short of impressive: a 40 under 40 honoree, a multi-award-winning cyber advocate, a captivating TEDx Speaker, a three-time published and award-winning children's book author, a prominent voice in LinkedIn's Cybersecurity Top Voice, a LinkedIn Learning instructor, and a dedicated board member at Black Girls in Cyber. Zinet had been on my radar for some time, and our paths crossed as we both pursued cloud certifications under the guidance of the same mentor. It wasn't long before I was captivated by her brilliance in authoring children's books in the field of cybersecurity. I marveled at how effortlessly Zinet seemed to balance it all, especially as a devoted mother of four. Her ability to wear so many hats is truly astounding. Beyond her remarkable achievements, Zinet is a constant source of inspiration. She has lent her support to me as the Founder of BGiC by joining our board, always displaying incredible kindness and unwavering dedication. Zinet, I am at a loss for words when I think of the depth of your accomplishments and the inspiration you bring to this project. Thank you for joining me on this journey, and thank you for believing in the vision. Your presence elevates this endeavor, and I am profoundly grateful for your partnership.

Each of you has left an indelible mark on this collective work, and I am eternally grateful for your unwavering commitment, dedication, and passion. Together, we have created something extraordinary, and I eagerly anticipate the positive impact it will have on the world of cyber and beyond.

With heartfelt thanks,

Talya Parker

Table of Contents

FOREWORD

Sharing The Mic In Cyber

By: Camille Stewart Gloster

This book offers solace, unity, and motivation for those who feel marginalized in the realm of technology and cyber. It is an invitation to discover a supportive community and the courage to amplify your voice. Moreover, it provides an eye-opening experience for those who haven't experienced being "othered" in this industry.

This book serves as the key we have long sought after, unveiling the secrets to cultivating a positive professional journey in cyber careers. Cyberspace comprises technology, people, and policy, each crucial in mitigating cyber risks. Navigating this ever-changing landscape requires understanding societal norms, culture, geopolitics, law, economics, personal security, national security, and international security in addition to the technology itself. What captivates me about the cyber industry is its intellectual rigor, broad applicability, multidisciplinary problem-solving, technical foundation, and the opportunities it offers society. I find fulfillment in aiding others, expanding access to services, driving societal progress, fostering opportunities, and safeguarding our lives and communities.

I have had the honor of working at the highest levels of government, serving as the first Deputy National Cyber Director for Technology and Ecosystem Security, the highest levels of industry, serving as the first Global Head of Product Security Strategy at Google and conducting revolutionary research resulting in the training of federal judges on their role in mitigating exfiltration of national security-related tech and IP through the courts. I am so proud of the career I am building and the impact I've made on the field and in the lives of individuals globally.

Looking in from the outside, it may seem like my journey into cyber was smooth and obstacle-free and that I easily found my community and support network within the industry. But that couldn't be further from the truth. Despite my passion and achievements, there are times when exhaustion, loneliness, and a sense of defeat consume me. I have contemplated leaving this path more than once. Why?

Because I am a Black woman with immigrant roots. The weight of being invalidated, isolated, scrutinized, and always having to go the extra mile just to stand at the starting line is overwhelming.

While navigating professional and academic spaces as the only one or one of a few has shaped my unwavering work ethic and empathy, it also becomes a burden that can crush one's spirit and make you yearn for the safety of spaces where you feel genuinely welcomed.

Work environments are already tough with their competition, lean resources, and high expectations, but to add the stress[1] and homogeneity[2] of an industry like cyber, it can be demotivating, to say the least. Additionally, I saw how groupthink and systemic bigotry can impact the industry's ability to innovate, address cyber risk, and recruit and retain talent. Applying the same security controls across communities and user groups may not yield the same or similar outcomes. Greater efficacy in cybersecurity requires

---

[1] https://www.zdnet.com/article/cybersecurity-leaders-want-to-quit-heres-what-is-pushing-them-to-leave/

[2] "And yet, minorities are grossly underrepresented in the industry. According to the Aspen Digital Tech Policy report, only 9% of cybersecurity experts are Black. About 8% are Asian and 4% are Hispanic." https://www.forbes.com/sites/forbestechcouncil/2022/09/30/minorities-and-the-cybersecurity-skills-gap/?sh=1f461cdd7f3f quoting https://www.aspeninstitute.org/wp-content/uploads/2021/09/Diversity-Equity-and-Inclusion-in-Cybersecurity_9.921.pdf

modifying or redesigning to consider and account for the unique needs, perspectives, and preferences of certain user groups, particularly historically underrepresented users, older users, or users with special needs. For example, if the primary or only means to add additional security is through two-factor or multifactor authentication, this could cause disproportionate harm to communities that cannot afford multiple devices, may be sharing a device with others, and are most often interacting exclusively on a cell phone. Understanding where controls fall short requires understanding individual communities and being attuned to the disproportionate harm that certain policies can have on them. [3]

This caused me to create the spaces and conversations I sought as I entered and began navigating the industry. #ShareTheMicInCyber[4] was just one of my efforts to create space in the industry and help address two of our most significant vulnerabilities as an industry and a nation - systemic bigotry and a loss of focus on people. #ShareTheMicInCyber, a volunteer-run movement, was

---

[3] https://www.fdd.org/wp-content/uploads/2023/04/fdd-memo-safer-together-inclusive-cybersecurity.pdf
[4] https://www.sharethemicincyber.com/

born during the early days of the COVID-19 pandemic and amid the fallout of the murders of Black Americans. Over a two-and-a-half-year period, the #ShareTheMicInCyber movement grew and evolved in ways that my co-founder Lauren Zabierek, co-host Katelyn Ringrose, and I could not have imagined. What started as a spark of an idea has grown into a global movement with various offshoots and a diverse community of supporters, participants, and organizations. It demonstrates in and of itself the power of community and diversity, particularly in this field where understanding people is integral to the work.

But while this movement has catalyzed essential conversations around race, racism, misogyny, and bigotry in cyber, helped bring people back to the center of cyber work, and created relationships between people that may not have been likely before such a movement. There is still so much work to be done.

In creating #ShareTheMicInCyber, I had the pleasure of meeting some of the most amazing humans and talented practitioners from a variety of backgrounds. The support and dedication from industry players at all levels helped restore my faith in the industry's desire for equity and inclusion, doubled my motivation, and I made several friends, including the women featured in this book. One of which is Talya Parker, the visionary behind this book. This driving force of a woman created an organization, Black Girls in Cyber, to diversify and amplify the industry within minority communities, shares her platform, and is now championing sharing the advice, counsel, and remarkable stories of 15 talented Black women cyber practitioners. I learn from this brain trust daily, and I am so glad she has captured their stories of adversity, triumph, entrepreneurship, and success. This book is doing the work to create space in the cyber industry, to share the mic (and more) in cyber, and, most importantly, to provide actionable advice for Black women and other marginalized practitioners and future practitioners.

As you dive into the stories of these remarkable Black women trailblazers, I hope that you truly feel seen, heard, and empowered to persevere in your journey through the cyber industry. Never forget your unique identity, keep people at the center of the work, and always strive to create room for others as you navigate this path. It's not just essential for your well-being, but it's a vital responsibility for the progress we seek to achieve. We are all cheering you on!

- Camille Stewart Gloster, Esq.

Camille Stewart Gloster, Esq. is an internationally recognized cyber, technology, and national security strategist and policy leader whose career has spanned the private, public, and non-profit sectors. She joined the Office of  the National Cyber Director from Google, where she most recently served as global head of product security strategy and, before that, as head of security policy and election integrity for Google Play and Android. Prior to working at Google, Camille led cyber diplomacy, technology policy, privacy, and technical policy areas as the senior policy advisor for cyber, infrastructure & resilience at the U.S. Department of Homeland Security (DHS). During her time at DHS, Camille led campaigns, international engagements, and policy development that bolstered national and international cyber resilience. For more information about Camille's career visit www.camillestewartgloster.com

Disclaimer: *Camille authored this foreword in her personal capacity and it does not reflect the views or opinions of her government employer or any affiliated organizations.*

Introduction

This inspired body of work that you are holding in your hand is a manifestation of nurturing your network, utilizing one's influence, and allowing your network to work for you. Never underestimate the power of building with the people around you. Unified purpose is an accelerator for massive growth and it is the framework for driving collective efforts forward.

This body of work is also a call to action for more Black women to see themselves in Cyber. With the increasing reliance on technology in all aspects of our lives, cyber has become a critical factor and concern for society at large. Communities of color, including Black communities, often face greater risks in the digital age, from surveillance to data breaches. Black women have a long history of advocating for and protecting their communities. From civil rights leaders like Fannie Lou Hamer to contemporary activists within the Black Lives Matter movement, we have shown an unwavering commitment to safeguarding the rights and well-being of marginalized communities. We must take up space in cyber and be in the position to ensure technologies and business models are designed to protect, rather than harm, these communities.

It is our hope that as you peel back each page, you become more aware of your power, and as you read each story that shares the unique pathway into cyber, you are able to realize your own potential within the myriad of cyber-related disciplines. Whether it be in security, privacy, online safety, data protection (e.g., encryption), or data governance - there are career options for you. Within these disciplines, there are additional skills that you may already have mastered that are transferable including strategy, training, operating model development, program management, risk management, compliance, engineering, product development, and technology implementation. The pathways and options are vast.

Sis, there is room for you at the table. We have made room for you. I hope our stories inspire you and showcase that we are Black women who dared to embark on a path without a blueprint, and because we had the audacity to believe that we could excel outside of our comfort zones, you have access to this book, our love letter, to you, that provides insight on how you can leverage your transferable skills and carve out a successful cyber path of your own.

CHAPTER 1

The Black Women in Cyber Collective
"An Inspired Vision for The Future"

By: Talya Parker

"Through a shared vision, we become architects
of a future that was once a dream; a vision
shared is a destiny achieved."

Born on the beautiful island of Jamaica, I absorbed the essence of community, relationships, and hard work from my parents and the people of my culture. At the age of eight, a new chapter began as my family embarked on a journey to the United States, seeking a brighter future. In my heart, I hold vivid memories of my mother's unwavering dedication as a new migrant. I watched her rise before the sun, prepare my sister and me for school, navigate city buses under the sweltering South Florida sun, and care for the elderly during her nine-to-five, all while pursuing her own dreams. Her brilliance always found a way to shine through, leading her to earn a Master's in Leadership and become an esteemed occupational therapist and a reverend clergy member. Her profound influence established the foundation for my own resilience, determination, and unyielding spirit.

In parallel, I was captivated by my father's exceptional skills as a carpenter, witnessed through his collaboration with my Uncle Paul. Juggling two jobs, he embarked on pre-dawn newspaper deliveries, returning home to ensure a warm breakfast for his girls, and then off again to his construction site. Despite my young age, my emotional intelligence was sharp, and I found myself a constant companion to my father during his summer newspaper routes, marveling at his boundless energy.

The indelible memory of my father's resilience remains, even after a horrific construction accident claimed his finger. Our migration from Jamaica to the US was nothing short of transformative. It instilled within me a deep well of resilience, an aptitude for adaptability, and an enduring reverence for the strength of relationships. These early adolescent experiences and the demonstrative qualities of perseverance, navigating ambiguity, and hard work have been instrumental in my journey toward becoming a leader in the field of cyber and privacy.

My path into Cyber was far from conventional. I studied abroad in Sydney, Australia during the summer prior to my college graduation, and again, post-grad in Shanghai, China, where I truly felt enriched by my experiences and the connections I made. Many members of my family and a few close friends thought I was nuts to travel so far alone for months at a time. Although I went alone, I came back rich in friendships and with an expanded network that was diverse, enriching, and influential; so much so, that connections made abroad were in attendance at my wedding.

ADAPTABILITY

In the dynamic realm of Cyber and Privacy, change is the only constant. New laws and updated standards regularly emerge, shaping the landscape. Your capacity to adapt to this ever-evolving landscape and cultivate fresh, cross-functional relationships to grasp the priorities of key business leaders will be pivotal to your success in what often proves to be an intricately ambiguous domain.

After earning my Bachelor's degree in Business from the illustrious HBCU, Florida A&M University, and completing my summer study abroad programs; I began working in banking. It was a good start, but I felt unfulfilled in my career and yearned for more. I confided in my friend and peer mentor, Raquel, about my frustrations. She introduced me to the world of Cybersecurity and Privacy, which was relatively unknown to most people at the time. With Raquel's guidance, I quit my job in banking and landed a four-month data Privacy internship at her boutique consulting firm. During undergrad, it had been a dream of mine to work for a Big 4 consulting firm, but when I graduated from college, I was met with rejection. During my freshman year, I found myself in a domestic violence situation that significantly affected my emotional and mental health. As a result, my grades plummeted, and although my latter years were filled with mostly As and some Bs, the weight of my freshman year experience continued to follow me. I was disappointed, and my confidence was shattered, but I didn't give up. This internship, although it was not a Big 4 firm, was the opportunity I needed to start. I decided to rebuild my network, my brand and put my energy into creating an impressive resume and LinkedIn profile, showcasing my study abroad and internship experiences.

AN UNYIELDING SPIRIT

Despite my previous bumps in the road, my journey unfolded from rejection to expeditious success, fueled by an unwavering determination to realize my dreams and a willingness to make the essential sacrifices. As a woman of color navigating this industry, rejection, isolation, and the feeling of being misunderstood have been recurring themes. Yet, your resilience to weather the toughest challenges, your unwavering determination to excel and be the brilliant presence in any room, coupled with an unshakeable spirit, will guide you through the rough patches and propel you towards flourishing when your moment arrives.

One day while perusing LinkedIn profiles, I stumbled upon a woman named Carla who worked as a flight attendant for a reputable airline. She wasn't a cyber professional, however, she worked with a company for which I was interested in pursuing. With nothing to lose, I decided to send her a message, hoping she would be willing to connect with me. To my surprise, she responded, and we agreed to meet in person at a Starbucks near the airport. When I arrived, Carla was already there, sipping on her coffee with a warm smile on her face. We began talking, and to my amazement, we hit it off right away. Our conversation had an effortless flow, and before I knew it, hours had passed. As we said our goodbyes, Carla mentioned that she had a friend who worked in international business and that she would love to connect us.

I didn't know what to expect, but I trusted Carla and decided to take her up on her offer. A few days later, she made the introduction, and to my surprise, her friend turned out to be a Partner at the same Big 4 consulting firm that had rejected me after undergrad. Carla's introduction had given me a foot in the door that I never thought was possible. Through her, I was able to build a genuine connection with the Partner and showcase my potential.

NETWORKING ADVANTAGE

Carla, a flight attendant, worked in a different industry from mine, but she turned out to be an invaluable resource. This situation underscores the importance of

---

> *not underestimating those in the room. Even if someone may not have a direct impact on your industry, you never know the extent of their network. Building trust is essential before people are willing to share their connections.*
>
> *"Networking is not about just connecting people. It's about connecting people with people, people with ideas, and people with opportunities."*
> *- Michele Jennae*

I knew that connecting with the Partner was my opportunity to make a lasting impression. I shared my goals and aspirations with him, hoping to glean some wisdom that would help me become more marketable and competitive in the industry. And oh my, did he deliver! He listened to me and provided me with a laundry list of tips and recommendations. With an attentive ear, I eagerly jotted it all down in my notebook. I took his advice to heart and went to work, determined to check off every item on the list. Over the next two years, I poured my heart and soul into my work, striving to improve my skills and build knowledge. When I reached out to the Partner again, I was thrilled to report that

I had done everything he had suggested. He was impressed with my dedication and perseverance and wasted no time inviting me to submit my resume. I had proven myself and gained his trust, and in return, he gave me access to his network. He introduced me to a female Partner who led an entire geographical region within the firm. Within two weeks, I found myself in the midst of a whirlwind of interviews, including a nerve-wracking trip to Houston for an in-person meeting. Despite the pressure, I felt confident in my abilities, knowing that I had worked hard to get to where I was. The following week, I received an offer that surpassed everything I had prayed for. To go from rejection to acceleration in just a few short years was surreal, and I was grateful for every opportunity that had come my way. This experience taught me that sometimes the best opportunities can come from unexpected places and that the power of networking should never be underestimated. With hard work, dedication, and a little bit of prayer, anything is possible.

CONSISTENCY

Consistency is the glue that holds us together, the rock we can lean on when the winds of change start to blow. This truth became evident during a chance meeting with the Partner at my dream company. Eager to absorb his wisdom, I recognized the importance of staying steadfast. I committed to following through on my obligations, approaching each day with unwavering dedication. This perseverance yielded results. In two years, I accessed opportunities that once felt unattainable. This lesson remains etched in my mind: consistency unlocks potential and fosters enduring relationships.

I'll never forget my first project as a Big 4 Cyber Security consultant. It was a daunting task, to say the least. I had been tasked with writing a comprehensive system security plan based on the stringent guidelines set forth in the National Institute for Standardized Technology (NIST) Security and Privacy Controls for Information Systems and Organizations 800-53. It was one of those situations where you either had to sink or swim; and swim I did, and as fast as I could. With grit and determination, I dove headfirst into the project, spending countless hours pouring over documents and researching best practices. As the days turned into weeks, and the weeks turned into months, I found myself becoming more and more adept at navigating the complex world of Cybersecurity. Before I knew it, not only had I developed and implemented multiple system security plans for multiple agencies, but I had become one of the top performers on my team. While my peers were often benched or seeking out new opportunities, I was juggling two or three clients at a time, managing complex projects with ease and efficiency.

Over time, I honed my skills in risk assessment, learning how to identify and evaluate potential security threats and vulnerabilities. I recommended and implemented mitigation strategies that were both effective and efficient, ensuring that my clients' data and systems were protected from harm. From there, my list of skills continued to grow. For almost five years, I worked in security & privacy consulting, serving a wide portfolio of clients across multiple service offerings and industries. The caliber of clients and the rooms that I was able to enter at such a young age excited and fired me up about the work I was doing. I had no idea that

Cybersecurity was so broad until I saw how the consulting world delivered its plethora of services. I gravitated mostly to work centered around Governance Risk & Compliance (GRC). Having the opportunity to sit with executives, handle the messaging, and support the decision-makers for security was work that allowed me to bring my skills to the forefront while also providing the fulfillment that I had been missing.

One year, I made the decision to pursue a promotion. My billable hours were off the charts, consistently receiving glowing feedback from partners and senior managers. I was one of the few consultants frequently double or triple booked on a single client, often responsible for training and even managing my peers, including my manager at times. I firmly believed that my dedication deserved compensation and recognition.

In the consulting world, you're typically assigned a coach or leader, usually a senior manager or partner, to advocate for you and provide guidance on advancement. I submitted my request for a promotion, only to receive the response, "you weren't ready." This conflicted strongly with the feedback and my extensive hours.

What do you do when the person holding your future in their hands refuses to acknowledge your worth? I decided to reach out to every partner, senior manager, or manager I had ever worked with, along with every internal community initiative and proposal I had contributed to, asking for recommendation letters that highlighted their reviews and feedback. It was an unprecedented move, as no other consultant was building such a comprehensive business case.

Within days, I compiled a compelling case for why I deserved the promotion. I also had another partner, a regional leader well-acquainted with my work, follow up with the decision-maker on my behalf. Even though they had already announced the promotions, I was determined to make it clear that I was indeed exceptional.

Behind closed doors, discussions took place, and the following week, I received the news of my promotion and a well-deserved change in title.

BE RESILIENT

I could have chosen the easier path of accepting defeat and acquiescing to his perception of where he thought I

---

should be. However, that marked the first instance in my life when I felt an unwavering determination to stand up for myself. The evidence was clear, the relationships were in place, and the undeniable value I brought was apparent. His astonishment was palpable when I successfully secured written commitments from numerous Partners and Senior Managers. He seemed to overlook the extent of my network and the comprehensive value I contributed to the firm, despite having shared these insights with him previously.
It's a testament to the importance of maintaining resolute and unwavering in advocating for what you rightfully deserve.

As I climbed the ranks in the cyber and privacy world, I decided to pursue a Master's in Cybersecurity from Brown University, after having already completed a Master's in International Business from Nova Southeastern University. Although I was thrilled to have been accepted to one of the top Ivy League universities in the world, being the only Black woman in my cohort was all too familiar of an experience, as it was a reflection of what it was like working in this field. But I didn't let that hold me back. Today, with over a decade of experience in privacy and security, I now possess a wealth of knowledge and experience that makes me an executive advisor and subject matter expert. I have worked with cross-functional teams to integrate security controls into system design and development, conducted vulnerability assessments; and led General Data Protection Regulation (GDPR) readiness activities, managing multiple privacy and security workstreams. My expert understanding of these topics enables me to provide sound guidance and insights to help organizations navigate complex privacy and security regulations. I have helped organizations to build a culture of privacy by design and more secure products for billions of users. With my unique blend of technical expertise, strategic vision, and leadership skills, I am now well-equipped to drive successful outcomes and deliver value to organizations seeking to enhance their GRC programs.

LEVEL-UP

In this space, it's all about embracing continuous learning. I'm all for diving headfirst into those tough projects, pushing through the discomfort, and not

---

shying away from asking questions or even stumbling a bit along the way. It's a fact, you've got to be exceptionally good, if not better, and then some. That's just the way it goes. But trust me, you've got what it takes with the right resources. Go after those certifications, pursue that degree, and don't hesitate to take on fresh challenges. You're teachable as long as you're coachable.

Today, I am excelling in my career as a cyber and privacy leader and influencer, doing work that I love and making a significant impact by raising awareness around opportunities for Black women to thrive within this industry. While my work is both rewarding and fulfilling, my journey has not been void of challenges along the way. As the only Black woman in many of the rooms I occupied, I often faced microaggressions and felt the weight of imposter syndrome as I worked to establish my brilliance in a space where my counterparts didn't look like me and had experienced the world quite contrary from the way I had as a first-generation immigrant. Despite the challenges of adjusting and acclimating to the environment, I learned to nurture my relationships and create spaces, such as Black

Girls in Cyber (BGiC) and the Black Women in Cyber Collective (BWiCC), to birth opportunities that were missing instead of simply complaining that they weren't there. I met the idea of lack with an abundant mindset and chose to be the change I wanted to see. I leaned into and leveraged the power of community to overcome obstacles of inclusion by establishing organizations that would serve as a hub of support, advancement, mentorship, and resources for career growth, for those who were coming behind me.

ARCHITECT OF CHANGE

I encourage you to be the the change you want to see. If there's a void, take the initiative to fill it. When you encounter obstacles, don't just attempt to leap over them; consider dismantling them entirely. You undeniably possess the capability, determination, and resilience required to shape the transformation your organization and the world require.

In 2020, the entire world shut down, causing corporations to pivot into web-based video conferencing as a primary mechanism to stay connected with their teams. I vividly remember being on a virtual call and realizing that I was the only Black woman not only in the room figuratively but literally the only Black face on the screen. This created a sense of urgency to do something to increase representation for minorities, specifically Black women who, like me, were capable, competent, and able to offer their gifts and talents in a vastly growing industry, "there goes the visionary again". Urgency fueled inspired action, and I founded, Black Girls in Cyber (BGiC Foundation), a non-profit organization, whose mission is to promote cyber, privacy, and STEM opportunities for women of color while increasing diversity within these respective fields. BGiC aims to achieve this by providing mentorship, scholarships, training, events, and community outreach.

The vision of BGiC is to create a pipeline of qualified women who can serve our communities in these critical roles. We believe we can inspire the next generation of leaders by fostering a supportive and inclusive environment and driving meaningful change in the industry. I recognized the power of vision and the change it can encompass when we back our ideas with action, intent, and deliberation. The beauty of vision is that it tends to expand our perspective, and as it widens, we see more possibilities. This book coupled with the Black Women in Cyber Collective is evidence that potential is amplified when the purpose is aligned. The inspiring collection of stories shared within this book is a reflection of a vision come true to bring women together and shine the light on their stories, contributions, and hard work. It's a sacred and intentional space where diverse voices and various perspectives can come together to shape the future of Cybersecurity and Privacy. As a visionary in cyberspace, I believe in the power of collaboration, effective relationships, and the importance of nurturing them.

In this cyber collective, I focus on cyber leadership, fostering community, and strengthening relationships for positive growth. My goal is to unite passionate leaders dedicated to impactful change and a secure, inclusive digital world. Together, we can leverage our collective expertise and experiences to drive innovation and shape the future of Cybersecurity and Privacy. That is my vision for BWiCC and the book you are holding.

BUILD YOUR TRIBE

There's something truly special about uniting and weaving our stories into a tapestry of memories that stand the test of time. It's this very essence that forms

---

genuine connections. Whether it's a shared passion, a mutual interest, or simply spending quality time together, engaging in meaningful pursuits lays the foundation for robust and lively relationships. Yet, it's not just about finding commonality - it's about being deliberate over the long haul. It's about dedicating the time and energy to be there, fully present, and fashion moments that will be treasured for years to come. Take that extra step to genuinely understand others, to partake in their triumphs and tribulations, and to establish a bond that defies both time and distance. When it comes to fostering enduring connections, never underestimate the influence of active involvement and the enchantment that unfolds when we unite to build enduring memories.

When I conceived the idea of inviting the most talented and accomplished Black women in the industry to embark on this collective co-authorship journey with me, I never imagined that all 15 of them would agree to participate. They all said, "YES!!" This experience has truly emboldened me to embrace my visionary nature and recognize my capacity to drive change as a leader, influencer, mover, shaker, and innovator. I possess a unique gift for bringing people together in any setting or circumstance, which I now consider to be my superpower. It empowers me to identify gaps and take courageous action to address them. The power of community, relationships, and leadership have been the foundational principles of my success. At the center of community and leadership are the people with whom we lead, influence, build, and grow. Relationships are often the bottom line of building anything substantial. As I've continued to elevate my career, establishing and effectively nurturing relationships have been key to my growth evidenced by my entry into the field of cyber. If you desire to advance in the way you lead or inspire connection within your community or organization, I encourage you to focus on your human capital by utilizing the key principles in this chapter.

My journey into Cybersecurity and Privacy has been unconventional but immensely rewarding. Anyone can succeed in this field, regardless of their background, as long as they are passionate, adaptable, and willing to learn. I am excited about the future of Cybersecurity and the role that I can play in shaping it.

Talya C. Parker

Privacy and Security Engineer Leader | Industry Change Maker

Talya C. Parker, a distinguished leader in the realms of Privacy and Security Engineering at Google, boasting an extensive career spanning over eleven years in the dynamic domains of Cybersecurity, Privacy, and Risk Management. Her expertise shines as she excels in Governance, Risk, and Compliance (GRC), having lent her skills to prestigious global entities such as Deloitte, Nike, and the Georgia Technology Research Institute (GTRI).

She is a proud alumna of the esteemed Florida A&M University, holds a Master's degree in Cybersecurity from Brown University and a Master's in International Business from Nova Southeastern University. Throughout her illustrious career, Talya has spearheaded multifaceted initiatives aimed at mitigating security and privacy risks, orchestrating compliance strategies, and ensuring adherence to stringent regulatory mandates. Her adeptness has enabled her to triumphantly lead complex projects across diverse industries.

Recognized as the "Cyber Visionary," Talya stands as the driving force behind The Black Women in Cyber Collective—a visionary endeavor that brings together a diverse spectrum of women of color to co-author this compelling book. Beyond her professional pursuits, Talya serves as the Founder of the BGiC Foundation, a powerful beacon for "Black Girls in Cyber." The organization is steadfast in its mission to champion diversity and inclusivity within the realms of cyber, privacy, and STEM fields, especially for women of color. BGiC delivers invaluable cyber and privacy career training, mentorship, networking, and job placement services, bolstering the empowerment of Black women globally and harmoniously bridging the gender and racial divides within the tech landscape. Through her foundation, Talya is unwavering in her commitment to cultivating a brighter future for Black women on a global scale.

In addition to her remarkable accomplishments, Talya is a celebrated author and a recipient of accolades for her outstanding contributions to her industry. She was honored as a nominee for the prestigious SANS Difference Maker Awards (DMA) and was bestowed with the title of "Diversity Champion of the Year" in 2022. The SANS Institute, the world's foremost authority on information and cyber training and certification, underscores the significance of her achievements. Talya has graced the stage as a distinguished speaker at an array of conferences, panels, and roundtables, including illustrious venues such as the White House ONCD, the National Security Agency (NSA), CISA's Cyber Summit, the Black Women in STEM Conference, numerous SANS events, Blacks in Technology, Junior Achievement (Florida), and the RSA Conference. Her voice has also resonated through various podcasts, where she ardently shares her zeal for nurturing the pipeline of women in the fields of cyber, privacy, and STEM.

Talya's journey stands as a testament to her unwavering commitment to excellence and her tireless efforts to uplift and empower women of color in the ever-evolving world of cyber. Her story is a compelling testament to the transformative power of determination and advocacy, inspiring a brighter and more inclusive future for all.

Linkedin: *https://www.linkedin.com/in/talyaparker/*

Website: *www.talyaparker.com*

CHAPTER 2

Cyber Evolution
"Pioneering Change From The Inside Out"

By: Dr. Mona Lisa Pinkney

When I began my career in cyber, there wasn't a defined career path. I had to create my own path and recognize the importance of being in control of my destiny. I started out as a Resource Access Control Facility (RACF®) security administrator. As a RACF® security administrator, I was responsible for protecting all system resources. This was in the late 1980s when the IBM mainframe was the computing system of choice.

As marketplace industries expanded, I evolved with the system security discipline. When cyber adopted a more holistic approach, our practices transitioned from being access control administrators where we focused on controlling the access people had to systems, to then working with software developers, and helping them think about their security infrastructure at the beginning of the development lifecycle, as opposed to the end. During the late 80s and early 90s, data security was often a final consideration in the development life cycle process.

Research analytics revealed that integrating security measures at the end of the software development life cycle was not only expensive, but software was better protected when system security was the core of its creation process. Understanding the core competencies of early-stage system security, my role evolved to what is now considered a cyber consultant. When the company I was working for, decided to relocate its Systems Engineering Organization from Washington, DC to Colorado Springs, Colorado, I made the difficult choice not to move. I sought out work that would allow me to utilize my industry expertise while still prioritizing my ability to remain close to my family. I eventually found work at a woman-owned company.

The primary focal point of our work was information security. The company had contracts with the Federal Deposit Insurance Corporation (FDIC) and the Resolution Trust Corporation (RTC). The RTC was created solely to resolve the scandal around the savings and loan crisis in which approximately one-third of U.S. institutions failed in a ten-year period. I interviewed for the role of an individual contributor, however, I was hired as the program leader, where I was charged with leading a team to develop cyber awareness training courses that were aligned to various disciplines within the growing information security industry.

We created specialized training for developers, engineers, and various other emerging competencies. As the program leader, I reported directly to the FDIC executive who spearheaded the program. When he was offered an opportunity with the oldest and most established insurance company at the time, he offered me the opportunity to work alongside him doing work that was similar to what we had done for the FDIC. I joined him in working for the company and worked there for almost five years. While at that company, I was given the opportunity to lead a laptop security project. At this time, the distribution and use of laptops was new for companies. My project was to determine how to distribute laptops securely and educate the end user on proper security practices. The project required me to travel with a team to our regional sites and conduct focus group sessions.

The CEO wanted to ensure what we developed would work not only at headquarters but scale throughout the company. This project provided me with a lot of visibility. While at our site in Denver, I received a call from HR advising me that the VP of my area wanted to create a job specifically for me. Surprised and excited about the opportunity, I eagerly shared the information with my husband. I accepted the challenge but first asked, "What would the VP do to ensure my success?" I knew I would give my all, but I needed assurance that he would mentor and support me, which he did. I successfully fulfilled my obligation and was very comfortable in the new and higher-level role. When the company offered the opportunity for people at my level and higher to pursue an MBA at their expense, I signed up. We were advised later that the company was being acquired by another Insurance Company. During this time, there were lots of mergers and acquisitions happening in the industry. Although many of the senior leaders left as soon as the deal was finalized, I remained during the one-year integration process because we were offered a lump sum bonus to stay. When my year's commitment was completed, I joined my mentor and colleagues at an on-line trading company and remained there for another five years.

I believe in the power of relationships and quickly understood the importance of remaining connected to people in my profession. When my mentor, who I met early in my career, went to work at a North Carolina based financial institution, he recommended me for a position that he thought would be perfect for me.

The position required someone with a computer security and project management background. This was during the Enron scandal which revealed the governing vulnerabilities within financial institutions. As a result, new legislation was created called Sarbanes Oxley (SOX) which was a means to create finance controls as well as hold banks accountable.

I'm originally from North Carolina so it was a great opportunity for my family. I enthusiastically accepted the offer to lead what at that time was the number one risk program at the bank. While at the financial institution, I was responsible for implementing their response to SOX along with another regulation called the Gramm-Leach-Bliley Act (GLBA). These regulations required that all financial companies that were publicly traded had to be SOX and GLBA compliant. During the 2008 financial crisis, the financial institution was purchased by another financial institution. I again stayed on with that financial institution for a year after the acquisition to help facilitate integration. I eventually left to take a position at a London based financial institution.

While participating in the MBA Fellows Program at Loyola College in Baltimore, Maryland, I had the opportunity to travel to Southeast Asia to visit program graduates who were expatriates. During this time, I became interested in being an expat at some point in my career and discussed my desire with my mentor. When my mentor left the North Carolina based financial institution and went to work at a London based financial institution, we stayed connected. Staying connected to my mentor proved beneficial because that professional connection and mentorship afforded me the opportunity to work in London. My role with a London based financial institution expanded to include regular travel to France, Italy, Lithuania, Portugal, and Spain. Maintaining my U.S. residency and working hard to manage my family and growing career, I eventually returned to the U.S. permanently. One of the Executives from the London based financial institution went to work for a U.S. based athletic footwear and apparel company, as their Chief Information Officer (CIO). The company was expanding its Cybersecurity organization; I was highly recommended for the role of helping them with the buildout.

I have been with the athletic footwear and apparel company for over eight years. When I started, I was responsible for what we called our cyber program office, then I moved over to lead the Governance, Risk, Compliance and Geographies organization. I successfully led the company in establishing global information security teams and programs expanding from a team at our World Headquarters to teams in our Asian and European headquarters.

I have always been an advocate for Diversity, Equity, and Inclusion. I had a great working relationship with my direct manager who was equally passionate. In working with my direct manager he encouraged me to document a DEI Strategy that could be shared with other managers. He approved the strategy and gave me a DEI budget. In 2019, during a technology leadership off-site, two of my peers and I started discussing what we perceived as a lack of representation in the industry of people who identify as Black. After the off-site, we started discussing an initiative to create a community of belonging, increasing representation at all levels in global technology, and providing career development opportunities for people who identify as Black. In talking to the Chief Diversity Officer, it was suggested that we become a "chapter" under the Black Employee Network resource group that serves the entire company. From these conversations, the Black Employees in Technology (BEiT) network was born.

In 2020, during the amplification of social unrest and a call for change after the death of George Floyd, effective strategies to implement diversity, equity, and inclusion initiatives were in demand. This movement was a catalyst that propelled our 2019 petition for change forward. Understanding the need to station diverse hires in the United States, we pitched the idea to our Chief Digital and Information Officer (CDIO) to develop a site outside of World Headquarters for our diverse technology new hires, and he quickly embraced the proposal. Since we had already done our research and had established strong established relationships with Universities in Georgia that would allow us to recruit talent, we were able to quickly develop a plan.

In November of 2021, it was announced that we were going to open a Technology Center in Atlanta, Georgia and

I was selected as the Senior Site Leader. The Atlanta Technology Center encompasses what we call the four centers of excellence with cyber being one of our pillars along with logistics & supply chain management, artificial intelligence, and machine learning. We are also gearing up to roll out an innovation lab that will focus on extended reality, augmented reality, virtual reality, and certainly, artificial intelligence and machine learning.

Working with the athletic footwear and apparel company to develop and spearhead a monumental movement that not only creates jobs for historically underrepresented groups but also allows our organization to be at the forefront of diverse global perspectives and opportunities is beyond my imagination. I feel that my passion and my purpose have been realized. As a pioneer in information security, I have been able to hold a first-hand perspective on how market, social, and technological changes directly impact the evolution of cyber.

My success has been in large part a reflection of my ability to adjust to an ever-changing demand for increased data security and cyber strategy, program development, integration and implementation.

It was my determination, great mentors, and the support of my husband that allowed me to overcome every obstacle presented. As I have successfully navigated the many changes in the industry, I have maintained five personal principles that have had a direct and positive impact on my career and success in life. I call these five principles the Five Be's - Be relentless, Be fearless, Be connected, Be global, and Be authentic. I think these five principles can be beneficial to anyone seeking to successfully navigate the many changes life brings them.

Be Relentless

This principle is built upon the foundation of passion and purpose. I believe when passion meets purpose, you will not stop until your goals have been realized. I know that my purpose is to help and prepare the next generation of technology and cyber leaders to drive change as well as innovation as the discipline continues to evolve.

Be Fearless

As the information security pathway evolved, it created volatile career security. To prepare for the social, financial, and technology changes that often disrupt companies you should always be open to change. Being fearless is about asking questions, being open to new opportunities, and constantly seeking to learn something new. My approach required that I be willing to try new things and discover new ways to integrate my expertise. Being fearless allowed me to remain employable through numerous mergers and acquisitions. MCI, IMSI, USF&G, Wachovia, and Ameritrade are companies that I worked for that no longer exist or exist under a new name.

If you are reading this chapter, you are seeking to understand how you can continue to learn and grow. I recommend that you maintain personal marketability within your industry through continuous learning, nurturing relationships, and staying connected to solution-focused perspectives especially when companies are impacted by change.

Be Connected

When I began my career, I was not familiar with the term "mentor". After connecting with an executive from MCI where we collaborated on systems security initiatives, I would go on to follow and learn from him as we both navigated the downfall of companies, the acquisition of others, and the overall evolution of cyber. He was not only my mentor, but he was also my sponsor and advocate. I was able to get new jobs because he was in rooms that I had not yet entered trumpeting my expertise on my behalf. I benefited greatly from his guidance and advocacy.

Creating a professional network, while identifying mentors and sponsors can be beneficial to the trajectory of your career. Once you benefit from having mentors and sponsors, I recommend that you commit to paying it forward by mentoring and sponsoring others. I have been a beneficiary of the generosity of others and as a result, I have committed to paying it forward. As a token of my appreciation, today I mentor a vast group of men and women. Throughout my life's journey, I have benefitted from both personal and professional network connections. It is my goal to pay it forward through mentorship and sponsorship of underrepresented groups so they can achieve what they have not realized was available to them.

Be Global

I grew up in a small town in North Carolina. I explored the world through books which planted in me a deep desire to experience the world through travel. One of my early personal commitments was to visit all 50 US states and all seven continents. I wrote this chapter while in Africa. It has been a full circle moment to be sharing this message while exploring the beauty of the 7th continent in my journey. I have been blessed to travel to the continent of my ancestors as the final one. As you continue your professional career, it is important to focus on enhancing your skill sets by understanding different cultures because you are not only competing with people from your hometown but with qualified talented people from all over the world.

Be Authentic

Growing up, my grandmother would often say, "Don't try to be like anybody else, because everyone else is taken." Of the many things that she taught me, this phrase left a lasting impression on me and my relentless endeavor to be the Me that only I can be. Throughout my career, I found myself at the receiving end of life-changing opportunities that my unique experiences, relationships, and understanding of the industry afforded me. Many times, I was in the right place, connected to the right people, and equipped with the right skills to leverage opportunities. I think it is important for you to know who you are, focus on your strengths, build upon your skills, and maintain an authentic desire to keep learning.

The decisions I have made along my career path have been the driving force of my destiny. I was able to withstand the many changes and challenges within data security. Whether it was the impact of a challenged financial services industry or a global athletic footwear and apparel company that dared to invest and implement diversity initiatives during a time when the world was experiencing the chaos of a global pandemic compounded with a demand for social change. I was coachable and able to effectively nurture long-term mentorship and advocacy. I was an expert in my own right by staying at the cutting edge of change within my discipline. As you embark on your career in cyber, or build your personal brand to establish and further market your expertise, know that you have the power to pioneer change, meet problems with resolve, make a positive impact in the lives of others, and contribute to the advancement of digital solutions.

Dr. Mona-Lisa Pinkney

Cyber Executive / DEI Advocate

Dr. Mona-Lisa Pinkney is a Cyber Executive with over 25 years of experience working at Fortune 500 companies. Dr. Pinkney strives to bridge technology and diversity through mentorship and sponsorship to underrepresented groups interested in pursuing a career in technology. She is a Global and Local Keynote speaker, named as one of the Top 30 Most Admired Minority Professionals in Cybersecurity by SeQure World Magazine. She is also the recipient of the 2019 Maryland Innovation & Security Institute's (MISI) Contemporary Women in STEM award and was listed as a Woman to Watch in Cybersecurity in Forbes Magazine.

As the recipient of four degrees and four certifications, Dr. Pinkney considers herself a lifelong learner and seeks to help others interested in pursuing college degrees and certifications in the technology field. In an effort to give back to her community, Dr. Pinkney provides a college scholarship to students graduating from her hometown high school. Dr. Pinkney also created an Endowment Fund in the College of Engineering at her Alma Mater, North Carolina State University.

Dr. Pinkney is a founding member of Black Women in STEM 2.0, an organization dedicated to supporting, promoting, and aspiring Black Women in STEM careers, as well as advocating for equitable and inclusive workplace environments that nurture diverse talent. Dr. Pinkney also serves on the Women in Cybersecurity (WiCyS) Equity Advocacy Committee (EAC), the Trustee Board at Florida Memorial University (the only HBCU in South Florida), the College Football Hall of Fame, and the Board of Directors for the Tech Talk Association (nonprofit arm of Black Women Talk Tech).

CHAPTER 3

I.T. Like Me
"The 3 C's of Cyber Career Success"

By: Deidra Phyall

"Diversity should matter, even in Public Service. My commitment to public service stems from my ability to change the diversity status quo and make a fundamental difference in the lives of others while providing awareness and access to opportunities that celebrate and amplify the talent and expertise of Black women in cybersecurity careers."

As you navigate life, there will be moments that define you, shape your beliefs, affirm your faith, and fuel your personal mission. These experiences serve as inspiration for us to seek purpose and pursue meaningful work. On my journey, I sought out work that allowed me to bring my unique skills, interests, and talents to the table.

During a period when information, computer science, and technology careers lacked diversity, my personal mission was motivated by a profound yearning for connection and acceptance. Due to the absence of individuals who shared my identity, navigating through this career track became a challenge. This challenge served as a catalyst for me to confront and question stereotypes, biases, and prejudices within the industry. Throughout this mission, I embraced a mindset of exploration and fearlessness, willingly venturing into uncharted territories. Remaining true to myself, I sought to carve out my path and redefine the boundaries of what was possible. I came to realize that the power to shape my reality and destiny fell solely on me, and it was through perseverance and determination that I could find my rightful place in the cyber landscape. *Representation matters!*

Now, as a passionate and dedicated leader, influential figure, and mentor in the cyber industry, I am deeply committed to cultivating a sense of community and fostering meaningful connections while making significant contributions to the field. My personal mission centers around creating and preserving opportunities for Black women to excel in spaces where their talents and skill sets bring immense value, particularly in non-traditional roles where their representation has been lacking.

I discovered my passion for technology early on as a young girl who had fallen in love with computers. I was enamored with the way they were built, how they were used, and their ability to process information so quickly. I grew up in North Carolina, where I attended predominantly white public schools. While I had access to well-resourced schools, I often faced ostracization accompanied by onliness as a result of being one of very few Black female students - whether it was the only Black person in a class, the only Black voice in a discussion, or the only Black girl interested in computer and technology related topics.

Given my unique experience and feelings of isolation, as my senior year approached, I developed a strong desire to enroll in a Historically Black College and University (HBCU). I wanted to be surrounded by and connected to other young, Black, and gifted scholars who loved Information Technology, *(IT) like me*. I went on to attend Winston-Salem State University (WSSU) where I majored in Management Information Systems (MIS). The illustrious Winston-Salem State University student body and staff created an atmosphere that felt like home. I experienced a profound sense of belonging and flourished throughout my academic journey. My time at WSSU presented opportunities that broadened my understanding of diversity and how to wholeheartedly embrace it from my perspective. Embracing diversity goes beyond mere acceptance; it entails the richness of diverse perspectives that emerge from individuals' distinct life experiences. It grants us an invaluable chance to learn from those who bring different perspectives, shaped by unique backgrounds.

The sense of connection, community, and diversity that I experienced during my academic journey sparked a deep desire within me to pursue employment where my primary goals include making a significant impact on a purpose-driven mission, engaging in impactful work that enables me to make a difference, and cultivating an environment where every individual feels heard, valued, and supported. Fearlessly amplifying my voice and embracing new possibilities, I have been able to fuel my passion, inspire transformative change, and establish a positive influential presence within the IT industry.

I currently work as a Senior IT Security Specialist within the Federal Government, renowned as the largest employer in the United States. Over the past 16 years, my professional career has been devoted to public service, with a specific emphasis on Information Technology. Within the last 5 years, I have shifted my focus to specialize in the field of cyber.

Throughout my career, I have taken on diverse roles within the field of IT and cyber. These roles include Software Tester and Developer, Liaison for Cyber Metric Reporting, Cyber Workforce Developer and Manager, Cyber Risk and Analysis Analyst, Cyber Policy and Strategy Planner. Having experience in various cyber roles, I discovered my career "sweet spot" where my passion and skills perfectly aligned.

It was in the role of being a Liaison for Cyber Metric Reporting that I realized cyber was not merely a profession but my true calling. This role involved bridging the gap between cyber experts, IT professionals, stakeholders, and managers while assessing the organization's business goals and cyber posture. Utilizing an array of cutting-edge tools and technologies, I discovered my love for data analysis, reporting, education and awareness, and how to align cyber policies, strategies, and objectives to enhance security measures and cyber posture improvements. This role was engaging yet challenging. I was able to provide valuable insights and recommendations to enhance the agency's security posture. The intricate process of monitoring, analyzing, and reporting not only appealed to my technical expertise but also aligned with my mission to give back and contribute to the greater good.

As I continued to work in this role, my passion for the field grew. It was in this role that I thrived, giving my utmost dedication and commitment, knowing that I was fulfilling my purpose, merging my passion, and making a tangible difference in the world of cyber. The constant pursuit of professional growth and expertise led me to pursue a Master of Science in Cybersecurity and Information Security from Capitol Technology University in Laurel, Maryland, subsequently obtaining several relevant certifications.

As a Senior IT Security Specialist in the Federal Government, I have encountered numerous instances where I was the only person of my background or ethnicity. In the early stages of my career, people of color were significantly underrepresented in the industry. Recognizing the immense talent and potential within the Black community, I became determined to enhance our representation in corporate and government tech spaces. My goal was to foster increased diversity and inclusion in the realms of digital information, transformation, and implementation. Based on recent studies, the representation of Black/African Americans in the Total Federal Workforce is approximately 18.19%, with 11.66% holding positions at the Senior Executive Service (SES) Level. Among women, they constitute only 44.44% of the Total Workforce, and 37.85% occupy positions at the SES Level. These statistics are sourced from the Office of Personnel Management (OPM) Government-wide DEIA Annual Report for 2022[5], as well as Executive Order EO 14035[6]. Furthermore, according to the Aspen Digital Tech Policy report, the representation of Black cyber experts stands at only 9%, while women make up 24% of the cyber field. These figures are sourced from the "Diversity, Equity, and Inclusion in Cybersecurity" report by Aspen Digital, a division of the Aspen Institute, published in 2021.

---

[5] "Government-wide DEIA: Our Progress and Path Forward to Building a Better Workforce for the American People," Office of Personnel Management, February 15, 2023.

[6] U.S. President. Executive Order. "Diversity, Equity, Inclusion, and Accessibility in the Federal Workforce, Executive Order 14035 of June 30, 2021." Federal Register 86, no. 123 (June 30, 2021): 34593.

Over the last several years I have collaborated with leadership executives in the federal tech space to emphasize the significance of fostering diversity and creating opportunities for entry-level cyber careers. One program that resulted from this collaboration included a 24-month training program that promotes diversity and empowers new hires within the General Schedule (GS-5 through GS-12) ranks. The program provides customized learning experiences and career opportunities in the Cyber workforce, with the goal of enabling participants to develop essential skills, discover their niche in the field of cyber, and thrive in their professional careers. Although progress has been made in the industry in terms of diversity, equity, and inclusion initiatives, there is still a long way to go. I did not want to limit my efforts to just the federal government landscape, so I sought out like-minded individuals with a vision to drive diversity in Cyber. I was able to discover The Black Girls in Cyber (BGiC) Foundation and became completely inspired by its mission, vision, and goals. As a non-profit board member and Director of Mentorships at Black Girls in Cyber, I oversee initiatives promoting diversity and industry awareness in cyber and privacy. Our mentorship program bridges the gap between aspiring professionals and seasoned experts, empowering Black girls in their cyber endeavors.

> *"The only limit to the height of your achievements is the reach of your dreams and your willingness to work hard for them." - Michelle Obama*

While the conventional pillars of cyber, known as Confidentiality, Integrity, and Availability (CIA), hold great importance, I have personally discovered three principles that have profoundly impacted my career growth, development, and purpose within the cyber industry. These principles, referred to as the "*3 C's of Cyber Career Success*," have been instrumental in shaping my professional path.

1) **Community-** Simply put, success is not achieved in a silo. It truly takes a village to drive one toward their ultimate potential. No matter how great you are individually, your potential success is measured by aligning your resources to achieve a common goal. As a Black woman in a white, male-dominated industry, it's important to connect and build a community of support that offers guidance, advocacy, and acceptance. My career experiences have taught me the importance of creating

diverse environments. While we work to make room for those who look like us to have a "seat at the table", it is wise to also connect with and learn from those who are already in the room and are established and well-connected within their respective careers. Your white male colleagues can serve as allies and offer valuable mentorship along your career path. Once progress and success are achieved, it is important to extend a helping hand to those who follow in your footsteps, uplifting and ensuring support for the next generation.

To establish or engage in a community, there are several approaches you can take:

a. Organize cyber events: Take the initiative to arrange workshops, webinars, or seminars focused on cyber. These events can cover a diverse range of topics, catering to both beginners and those interested in advanced techniques for combating cyber threats. In my current position, we hold a weekly gathering every Monday called "In the Know" where my team and I discuss the latest cyber threats, IT developments, and any noteworthy occurrences in the IT/Cyberspace. The session typically lasts for 15 minutes.

b. Create online groups or forums: Establish virtual communities where you can share knowledge, ask questions, and engage in discussions related to cyber. For instance, you can create an online forum or social media group dedicated to cyber topics. Additionally, consider starting a cyber-themed podcast, such as "Do We Belong Here," where you can interview experts and share insights.

c. Collaborate with existing communities: Join forces with other communities and organizations to expand your impact. Look for established communities like Black Girls in Cyber, Black Girls Hack, Women Society of Cyberjutsu, or Empow(H)er and collaborate with them on joint initiatives, events, or knowledge-sharing efforts. By leveraging their existing networks and resources, you can broaden your reach and create a more inclusive and diverse community.

Embarking on a cyber career, whether you're a beginner or an experienced professional, can feel overwhelming at first. It is crucial to recognize that confidence grows with competence, and you're not alone on this path. Take the proactive step of cultivating a supportive community, forging meaningful connections, honing your skills, and seeking a sense of belonging. Remember that you can learn from and inspire one another through valuable connections.

2) **Collaboration-** There is a well-known African proverb that reminds us, "If you want to go fast, go alone, but if you want to go far, bring your tribe." While pursuing personal ambitions may yield quick results, community-focused endeavors require unified efforts to accomplish significant goals. Collaboration holds the power to transform individual ideas into powerful movements, amplifying dreams and propelling change forward. One key aspect of collaboration in the cyber field is information sharing and industry collaboration. By actively participating in knowledge exchange, attending training sessions, and engaging in conferences, you can stay updated on the latest trends, threats, and solutions. This continuous learning approach is vital for maintaining a strong foothold in the ever-evolving landscape of cyber. Another example of collaboration is cross-functional training. This can be done both internally and externally in the workplace. Find

someone in a different field of interest than you. Reach out to someone in IT, legal, compliance, risk management, etc., and leverage their expertise and perspectives to foster a holistic approach. This allows you to address vulnerabilities from various angles. Reflecting on your journey, it is essential to identify those who share your vision for change. By joining forces with like-minded individuals and organizations, you can increase the collective impact and achieve meaningful results. Collaboration is a fundamental element of success in the cyber field. By embracing collaborative practices, information sharing, continuous learning, and aligning with those who share your goals, you can make a significant impact and contribute to a more secure digital landscape.

3) **Contribution-** As you continue to embark on your growth journey, it is vital that you remain diligent in looking back and giving back, as it is through collective efforts that we can forge ahead, grow, and thrive. Contribution is not just about charity; it is equally about connection. To truly make an impact and drive change, it is important to stay connected to the cause and understand

the challenges faced by others. Mentorship should be seen as a mutually beneficial partnership, where you seek guidance, you also become a source of inspiration for those who follow in your footsteps. Mentors play a pivotal role in unlocking your untapped potential. As you build connections, consider how you can positively contribute to the industry. One way to contribute is by supporting causes, programs, and initiatives within your community or organization that align with your values. Reflect on how you can make a positive difference in the lives of others. Contributions can take various forms, including offering your time, talent, or resources to support continued growth and development in areas that matter to you. But what if you are new to the field and have limited knowledge of cyber? Start by staying informed and up to date on the latest cyber threats, trends, and best practices. Regularly read security-related blogs, news articles and attend webinars to enhance your knowledge. Participating in hackathons or competitions where you collaborate with others to solve real-world cyber challenges can provide valuable experience. Volunteering is another excellent way to contribute. Volunteering not only allows you to give back to the community but also provides you with opportunities to learn and grow in the cyber field. Seek mentors who can guide you on your journey and consider pursuing certifications in the specific domain of cyber that interests you. These certifications will help you gain expertise and stay competitive in the field. By actively contributing to the cyber field, you play a vital role in improving overall security for individuals, organizations, and society.

The 3 C's: Community, Collaboration, and Contribution are the foundational principles of career success and advancement. They provide a framework for making a lasting impact and leaving a legacy of reaching back and supporting others in any industry. Remember this journey is yours to embrace, so strive to be the best version of yourself, discover your passion, invest in your personal growth, seek out mentors, foster meaningful relationships, and build a strong network. You belong in Cyber! Success alone is not about your personal achievements, it is about giving back, fostering connections, and contributing positively to the community at large.

Deidra A. Phyall

Senior IT Security Specialist | Federal Government

Deidra A. Phyall's background spans more than 16 years in the Information Technology (IT) sector. Her wealth of experience encompasses a diverse spectrum of IT domains, ranging from software development, requirement and risk management, data visualization, analytics, Federal Information Security Management Act (FISMA) compliance and monitoring, information security, strategic planning, reporting, training, and development.

Deidra holds a Master of Science degree in Cyber and Information Security from Capitol Technology University, and she achieved a Bachelor of Science degree in Management Information Systems from Winston-Salem

State University (WSSU). Alongside her educational achievements, Deidra is the Founder of Mentorship Maverick and holds a prominent role as a non-profit board member and Director of Mentorships at Black Girls in Cyber (BGiC) (www.blackgirlsincyber.com).

In her current role as Senior IT Security Specialist within the Federal Government, Deidra's core focus is on cyber strategic planning, reporting, education, training, and workforce development. Driven by a passion for volunteerism and mentorship, Deidra dedicates her time to mentoring young women in IT and STEM fields. She strongly believes in giving back, paying it forward, and serving others. Deidra is an active member of Alpha Kappa Alpha Sorority, Incorporated, and holds leadership positions in various organizations, including NextGen Network, Collegiate Directions, Federal Employee Education and Assistance Fund (FEEA), Union Church, Young Government Leaders, WSSU National Alumni Chapter, League of United Latin American Citizens (LULAC), and the Association for the Improvement of Minorities (AIM). Throughout her professional journey, Deidra has received several accolades and awards, notably including the

Leading Change Award in Diversity, Equity, and Inclusion for Women Who Code, SANS Difference Maker Mentor of the Year Award, recognition as one of the 21 Women in Cyber and 1 Million Women in STEM, the NextGen Public Service Award for Innovator of the Year, and her induction into the WSSUNAA Hall of Distinction. She has also been honored as a WSSU Forty Under 40 recipient.

Beyond her professional pursuits, Deidra leads a fulfilling life as a devoted wife to her husband, Ptolemy and mother of two daughters, Sage Noelle and Steele Ivy-Grace. Her personal interests include kickboxing, traveling, and exploring her passion for food.

Connect with Deidra:

https://linkedin.com/in/deidraphyall

CHAPTER 4

Decoding Your Cyber Potential

By: Tanneasha Gordon

D ecoding is a crucial skill set to have in cyber and privacy. It allows experts to better understand complex systems and identify vulnerabilities that can be exploited by attackers. Decoding refers to the process of breaking down complex systems, networks, or codes to better understand vulnerabilities and potential weaknesses.

Decoding is also crucial in cryptography, which involves encoding data so that they can only be read by someone with the proper decryption tool; network traffic analysis, which involves decoding the data that flow between devices on a network to identify potential threats or suspicious activity; and malware analysis, which involves deciphering the code of malicious software to understand how it works and how it can be detected and neutralized. Just as complex systems and information can be decoded to uncover vulnerabilities, identify threats, and identify risks - as Black women in cyber, our potential can also be decoded. Here are some keys to decoding and deciphering your cyber potential:

I. Unlocking Your Potential

Everyone has potential. Potential is your capacity for growth, development, and ability to advance given the right circumstances. I believe your potential is shaped by what you have been exposed to during your early childhood and development stage of life. I believe it is shaped by what sparks you, what interests you, and what compels you. Potential is shaped by your talents, gifts, and how you choose to use those things. With the confluence of these things, potential always exists and we are readily presented with opportunities to spark our potential, pursue our potential, and unlock our potential.

> ### Cheat Code #1: Catalog Your Inspirations Early
> Your earliest inspirations can be a helpful starting point for identifying your passions and interests, but it's important to recognize that your aspirations may have evolved over time. When cataloging your earliest inspiration, it's important to be specific and thoughtful. Don't just think

about the things you enjoyed as a child or teenager, but also consider why you enjoyed them and what qualities they had in common. Were you drawn to creative pursuits? problem-solving challenges? or helping others? By understanding what inspired you early on, you can gain insight into the things you are passionate about and the things you are most interested in and potentially identify career paths that align with both.

I was seven years old, and it was career day in my second-grade class. I was wearing my favorite blue overalls, but it was nothing compared to the visiting attorney's black trench coat and top hat. I was completely captivated by his presence. Before that day, I dreamed of being a figure skater or a mermaid. But from that day on, I knew I wanted to be a lawyer—and a very well-dressed one.

Another career day that left a lasting impression on me was when I was in the 5th grade and a banker taught us how to balance a checkbook. I didn't leave wanting to be a banker, but the importance of being able to earn money and manage my expenses was not lost on me. However, in elementary school my only "income" was allowances, and my only "expenses" were snacks and Goosebumps and The Baby-Sitters Club books. To offset my expenses, I started working in the school library during book fairs in exchange for free books from my librarian. These experiences, combined with watching my mom work two jobs, shaped my work ethic as well as my relationship with money.

These are some of my earliest childhood memories that inspired my interest and intrigue in potential future career paths. I had the potential to become a lawyer, model, librarian, or banker; but it was my desire to be a lawyer that carried me through my entire academic career—from elementary school through graduate school.

In high school, I was immediately immersed in the field of law. I took classes taught by practicing attorneys and law school professors and competed in mock trial and moot court competitions. I was paired with an experienced attorney at a leading law firm in NYC through my school's mentorship program. This pairing expanded my worldview and allowed me to learn everything I could about the profession. Owing to this experience, I decided to attend Cornell University for undergraduate studies where I majored in Urban Studies with a concentration in Law & Society. This allowed me to delve deep into architecture, urban economics, city planning, transportation modernization, law, and public policy. I studied abroad in both Panama and Italy where I was able to analyze a myriad of economic development initiatives being explored by the local governments and provide policy recommendations on how to scale development, tourism, and economic activities.

Law school was still the plan, but when it was time to take the LSAT, I began experiencing recurring anxiety attacks. I had built my entire identity and life plan on becoming a lawyer; taking a 100-question test that would decide my future or unravel my plan started to consume me. When I communicated my trepidation to my college advisor, he suggested I stay an extra year and get my Master's in Public Policy (MPA) since I had already earned a number of credits as an undergrad that would be counted toward earning the MPA degree. He said this would give me extra time to prepare for the LSATs and an MPA would make me more competitive in the workforce. I agreed and dove right into the graduate school curriculum, which was split between government policy and business school courses.

Cheat Code #2: Explore Pathways and Adjacencies

Don't be afraid to go down the paths that present themselves. Lean into them. When exploring pathways and adjacencies, it's important to cast a wide net and be open to new possibilities. Don't limit yourself to traditional career paths or areas of study. Consider fields that may seem unrelated to your current interests but could offer new opportunities to apply your skills and knowledge. Look for connections and intersections between different areas of interest and explore how you can leverage your talents in new and exciting ways.

I ended up taking and acing several business school courses and joining the consulting club to learn more about the profession. Those experiences made me fall in love with consulting. I began to consider switching career paths but I felt like I was betraying a long-held dream of mine. So, I went to the place I always go when I need to do due diligence before making a decision: The Internet. I typed "law government consulting" in the search bar and one government consulting firm stood out to me: Booz Allen Hamilton. Then a series of synchronistic events took place confirming that I should switch paths and pursue this consulting firm.

One pivotal event was a dinner for a conference I was attending. There were two open seats next to me and the two strangers that sat next to me both worked for the very same consulting firm — one was a recruiter. I told her that her firm was my number one choice and she said, "When do you want to interview?" I eventually interviewed and got an offer on the same day. The way things lined up perfectly confirmed for me that I was on the right path, and I felt free to leave my lifelong dream of being a lawyer behind.

I started my consulting career in strategy and transformation where I learned to build multi-year strategies, design operating models, reengineer business processes using lean methodologies, and execute hypotheses and data-driven analysis for federal and commercial organizations. Two significant strategy projects that ended up being my entry into cyber and privacy involved developing a fraud detection program strategy and designing and implementing a breach response program. These adjacent projects created an opportunity for me to leverage existing skills, break into a new domain, and build new skills.

I have learned that having the ability to tap into your earliest inspirations and exploring pathways that reveal themselves to you can take you down the route designed for you to grow, self-discover, and tap into the potential that lies within.

II. The Power of Pivoting

A career in consulting, especially cyber consulting, requires professionals who can pivot based on market demands, client needs, the latest cyber threats, etc. Agility, grit, curiosity, and the ability to reinvent oneself are traits necessary to successfully pivot and properly adjust to career shifts.

One of the strongest and most instrumental pivots that I made in my career was pivoting from Strategy consulting to Cyber Risk consulting. At that time, from a consulting vantage point, strategy was considered "king." Strategies were often the lucrative deals that afforded consultants senior-level and board-level relationships. It was 2008, during the financial crisis when I realized that strategy was not going to be king in the near future. I thought, "If these banks had some of the best strategies and found themselves in the center of a financial crisis due to unmitigated 'risk', then the future will be predicated on risk management." That's when I decided to pivot from Strategy to Risk.

Cheat Code #3: Be flexible and open to possibilities

Inventory your talents, capabilities, and aptitudes: When taking an inventory of your talents, capabilities, and aptitudes, it's important to be honest with yourself and avoid underestimating your skills and abilities. Take time to reflect on your accomplishments and think about what skills you used to achieve them. Consider seeking feedback from others to gain a better understanding of your strengths and areas for improvement. By understanding your unique abilities and talents, you can identify career paths and opportunities that align with your strengths and enable you to thrive.

Adjusting to the needs of the new market, I accepted a job at a leading cybersecurity professional services organization. Given my Strategy background, I led the charge in designing a number of Information Security Programs, Privacy Programs, and Enterprise Risk Management Programs. I worked on everything from executing risk assessments, requirements analysis, and developing cyber strategies to implementing privacy programs, security programs, development, security & operations programs, and privacy engineering capabilities. I was able to recognize and unlock a career in cyber when the market was not as mature as it is today.

The second most significant pivot I have made in my career was pivoting from Healthcare & Life Sciences to Technology, Media & Telecommunications (TMT). When I matriculated to management level, I primarily focused on Federal Health and Commercial Lifesciences, which provided me with an amazing lifestyle. I traveled when I wanted to; I loved my clients; my projects were both challenging and rewarding; and I even got to relocate abroad. I lived in the Netherlands for nearly three years in anticipation of the General Data Protection Regulation (GDPR) taking effect. It was an incredible experience that encouraged me to stretch my capacity to manage new opportunities. It also provided unanticipated insight. For example, while in Europe I developed a greater appreciation for Privacy as a fundamental human right. I was also able to see how 'ready' heavily regulated companies in Life Sciences and Financial Services were when it came to complying with complex regulations due to muscle memory these organizations developed after years of being heavily regulated. I quickly realized that our technology clients weren't ready for the plethora of digital regulations that GDPR would shepherd in. Once I had that realization, I decided to once again pivot, this time to TMT.

When I moved back to the US, I settled in northern California with no business relationships, no friends, and no family. Fast forward to today, five years later, I am a partner at a leading cybersecurity professional services organization leading our data, privacy and digital trust business in the United States. In my role, I oversee and shape a broad set of offerings related to data protection, data governance, privacy, and content compliance I am responsible for the growth and success of the business including profits & loss, building our go-to-market strategy, innovating our offerings, developing platform solutions in collaboration with our Alliance relationships, and all things talent management including empowering and developing our people. When I am not managing this business and serving our people, I am serving clients.

> **Cheat Code #4: Uncover Your Capabilities, Talents & Aptitude**
>
> *Inventory your talents, capabilities, and aptitudes: When taking an inventory of your talents, capabilities, and aptitudes, it's important to be honest with yourself and avoid underestimating your skills and abilities. Take time to reflect on your accomplishments and think about what skills you used to achieve them. Consider seeking feedback from*

others to gain a better understanding of your strengths and
areas for improvement. By understanding your unique
abilities and talents, you can identify career paths and
opportunities that align with your strengths and enable you
to thrive.

One thing I have learned is that your talents, capabilities, and aptitude aren't just uncovered and cultivated in your occupation or role at work; it is discovered and uncovered in all aspects of your life that require your time, commitment, and resources. During my time at Booz Allen Hamilton, I was able to advance my strategy, improve operations, and learn new skills that elevated my capacity. I was also able to build a foundation in privacy and security strategy. During this time, I started a non-profit organization that operated in both Zimbabwe and the United States. I then became a seed investor in two Black-owned start-ups, an independent public relations strategist for a small film company, and began building a real estate portfolio.

These extracurricular activities allowed me to cultivate a diversified set of skills that would later be very useful during a career pivot. Often time, the best way to identify and cultivate your talents is by continuously putting yourself in uncomfortable situations. This means taking on roles that may stretch you, asking for direct feedback from your peers and direct reports, and taking time to reflect on your strengths and areas of interest. It can be very effective to ask yourself critical questions like, "What do you enjoy doing? What comes naturally to you? What do you excel at?" Make a list of your skills and abilities and identify patterns and themes.

Career pivots often require deep self-reflection and acquiring new skills or knowledge. Embracing change and learning new things can stimulate personal growth, prompt transformation, and surface hidden talents. Making these transitions can be a vital part of unlocking your full potential and is not a one-time event but a continuous journey.

III. Consistent Pursuit of Excellence

When we dedicate ourselves to the pursuit of excellence, personal development, and service to others, we find that our true potential moves from being unlocked to untapped. Unlocked potential is analogous to finding the right door and turning the latch so that it is unlocked, but it's up to you to open it. Untapped potential is when you have unlocked and opened the right door and opportunities just pour in. I have found that these opportunities require a pursuit of excellence, drive personal development, or enable you to serve others. By focusing on doing our best, personal growth, and contributing to the greater good, we tap into a powerful source of motivation and fulfillment. As we strive for excellence, we build competence, credibility, and our brand. As we focus on our growth and development, we become attuned to our strengths and weaknesses. We learn to further cultivate the strengths and qualities that make us unique and identify strategic ways to lean on others where we are weak. We may discover that our skills and passions align in ways that make our work not just a job, but a calling. Whatever your calling might be, at its core and foundation, it will be to be of service to others.

Cheat Code #5: Practicing excellence

Being authentically yourself should be the default. Establishing a personal brand such as a servant leader, focusing on qualities like reliability, trust, service, and excellence, naturally leads to increased followership, earnings, and overall impact. Tactics for staying on point and becoming indispensable:

→ Be known for something

→ Stay out front and ahead

> → Demonstrate value
>
> → Show-up & Show-out
>
> → Stay Ready so you never have to get ready

A profession in cyber as a Black woman doesn't allow much room for slackers, mediocrity, or prolonged instances of not meeting the bar. In cyber, not being on top of your game can mean the integrity of an entire sector or hospital system, the safety of everyday products, or national security. Second chances are a luxury in our field and because we are a rarity, excellence must be our default.

There are some people who can walk into a room and command respect because of their position, who they are, or their brand. However, to become one of those people and for your brand to carry that amount of weight it takes work. As a professional service leader and consultant, I like to think of myself and others in this space as professional cyber athletes. Just as athletes train, prepare, are coached, study, and care for their bodies - it's the same for cyber athletes. You shouldn't be waiting for your next training course or project to learn new skills. You need to be intellectually curious 100% of the time keeping ahead of trends. Anticipate what your clients need to know and keep a pulse on how your client's attack surface expands as their business models expand.

At a time when knowledge workers, especially those with technical skills, are being disrupted by Artificial Intelligence, practicing continuous development and exceptionalism will be critical. In the end, it will likely be those of us who are continuously in pursuit of excellence, staying ahead of the curve, and mastering the use of AI all while exercising high Emotional Intelligence (EQ) that demonstrates we are indispensable.

Cheat Code #6: Build Your Board

Who are your mentors and sponsors? Who are your table pounders? Do you have folks in your corner that won't just open doors for you and let you in the room, but will move people to create a seat for you at the table? Do you have a board of directors for your career? Who are those people?

Movers and shakers - those who are and have flourished in their careers - are always looking to bestow knowledge to younger professionals so that they are able to walk in wisdom. Wherever you are in your career, it's incredibly important that you seek out coaches, mentors, and sponsors;

and that you practice humility and submit to constructive feedback, guidance, and apprenticeship.

I learned very early in my career to treat my entire career as though it was its own entity - a corporation, to be exact. Just as a corporation has a CEO, operating functions or business groups, and a brand - so does my career. In this construct, I was the CEO of my career; my talents and capabilities were the operation functions; and my mission was the combination of my purpose and passion. Additionally, just as corporations are governed by a Board of Directors that keeps the CEO accountable, provides guidance and advice, and supports critical decision-making - our careers need the same level of governance. My personal board of directors consists of coaches, mentors, sponsors, and role models inside and outside my organization. My board members are professionals whom I respect and who have an invested interest in my career - some are even former clients. The coach, mentor, sponsor, and role model roles are often confused and conflated so I will explain the distinctions below:

→ **Career Coach** - A career coach is a professional who provides you with guidance and support as it relates to your career development and advancement. They assist you with identifying your goals, strengths, and areas for improvement, and offer insights into overall career management. They act as motivators, helping you stay on track and make informed decisions to progress in your career.

→ **Mentor** - A mentor is an experienced and knowledgeable individual who offers guidance and advice to less experienced individuals, known as mentees or protégés. Mentors share their expertise, provide valuable insights, and serve as a sounding board. They offer a safe space for you to discuss challenges, seek advice, and learn from a mentor's experiences. The mentor-mentee relationship is often characterized by trust, support, and the transfer of skills, knowledge, and wisdom from one generation of professionals to the next.

→ **Sponsor** - A sponsor is a senior-level professional within an organization who actively advocates for and supports the career advancement of a more junior employee. Sponsors go beyond providing advice and guidance; they use their influence and networks to create opportunities for you. This may include recommending you for promotions, high-profile projects, or leadership positions. Sponsors help individuals navigate the corporate landscape and actively work to remove barriers to their career progression. The fascinating thing about sponsors is that you may not know who they are or have frequent touchpoints with them - but they are aware of your potential and proactively betting on you. They recognize your potential and are batting for you in the background.

→ **Role Model** - A role model is someone who serves as an exemplary figure, inspiring and influencing others through their behavior, achievements, and values. Role models can come from various aspects of life, including personal, professional, or public figures. In a career context, a role model is often someone whose career trajectory, work ethic, or ethical standards serve as an inspiration to others. They demonstrate what is possible through hard work, dedication, and integrity, and they encourage others to strive for similar success. Your coach, mentor, and sponsor can also be a role model - it's all up to you.

These roles play essential parts in your career development and growth, each contributing unique forms of support and guidance.

> **Cheat Code #7: Be of service to others**
>
> *By serving others, we gain a deeper understanding of the world around us and our place in it. We see the impact we can have on the lives of others, and we recognize that our purpose lies in making a positive difference in the world. In what ways do you serve others?*

If you work within the confines of a company, firm or organization, it is a prerequisite that you know and understand its overall strategy, how cyber risk impacts that strategy, and how you can be in service of that strategy. If not to a company or firm's strategy, you should be in service to a mission or an idea that is bigger than you. As a cyber professional or consultant, serving others means helping your clients achieve their goals as well as helping them protect their assets and sensitive information. It means putting their needs first and delivering exceptional service that exceeds their expectations.

When deciding on where to play whether it be industry, sector, clients, or a field within cyber I found that my career always had a higher potential for advancement when I positioned myself as a servant leader. This mindset gave my brand and career trajectory a boost because I was always speaking to and solutioning for challenges and topics that helped others achieve their personal goals, their business objectives, or regulator expectations. What I learned is that we are positioned to thrive in places where our talent and market demands collide to serve other than ourselves. I truly believe that when I'm walking in my purpose or God's plan for my life it feels like surfing and catching a wave. It takes practice and dedication to be able to do so, but when I do, I know it's because I am moving with the current. However, if you're unable to catch any waves or constantly battling against the current, ask for help, get your footing, and execute the cheat codes outlined in this chapter to decode your potential. Once you have done that, get back out there and live up to your potential.

Tanneasha Gordon

US Data & Digital Trust Business Leader | Deloitte & Touch LLP

Tanneasha is a recognized cyber leader with over 17 years of experience advising large global organizations on privacy, content compliance, data governance, and data security. As a trusted advisor to her clients, she's usually in the trenches with senior leaders advising on complex compliance transformations that involve redefining governance models, rearchitecting products and platforms, revamping policies, revising controls, and redesigning operating models. Tanneasha is a forward-thinking technologist who keeps a pulse on emerging trends and technologies to help organizations anticipate and navigate disruption, threats, and opportunities to their business models and product roadmaps. She is a go-to-leader in times of crisis (e.g., data breach) and change (e.g. new regulation), with a demonstrated track record of developing effective remediation measures, interpreting complex requirements, assessing regulatory readiness and risks, pivoting product strategies, implementing 1 leading data solutions, and developing defensible strategies.

Tanneasha has been featured in multiple recognized media outlets including but not limited to the Wall Street Journal, Vox, Daily Mail, Reuters and Adage. She is a renowned cyber executive and highly sought-after speaker as well as a National Association for Female Executives (NAFE) Women of Excellence award recipient. Tanneasha sits on the board of Black Girls in Cyber, a non-profit focused on empowering and nurturing the talents of women of color in cyber, privacy, and STEM fields.

She also founded a non-profit in 2008 called, The Zimbabwe Education Fund (ZEF), dedicated to providing Zimbabwean orphans and underprivileged children the means to attain a quality education and acquire practical life skills. ZEF's mission is to address the barriers orphans and underprivileged children have accessing education and to engender leadership. The organization was transitioned to a local church in 2015.

Tanneasha also sits on the Leadership Council for Tipping Point - a grant-making organization aiming to break the cycle of poverty for people in the San Francisco Bay Area whose income level is too low to meet their basic needs.

Tanneasha is an adopted parent, a self-proclaimed sci-fi junkie (and currently writing her first sci-fi novel), an avid traveler, and recovering fitness fanatic.

LinkedIn

https://www.linkedin.com/in/tanneasha-gordon-3586b56/

CHAPTER 5

Create YOUR Cyber Cycle of Success
By: Mari Galloway

I entered the tech and cyberspace as a government contractor with Accenture in the fall of 2009, which, from a personal standpoint, I low-key hated. I had no clue what I wanted to do, but I got my foot in the door because of my mom. She was interviewing at the company, and let the recruiter know I had just graduated with a business degree in computer information systems. While she is my mom, she is also a part of my professional network, which is very important to establish and maintain throughout your career.

Most of my roles were technical and required me to understand technology and how people interact with it. If you don't know, government contracting is an interesting place to be as a contractor, but it has its perks. I ended up leaving the government to pursue roles that offered more flexibility and experience around cyber and tech. Around 2016, Casino security became my jam, someplace I never imagined working. This shift brought me to Las Vegas to help build a Vulnerability Management program and eventually move into Security Architecture.

Vulnerability Management entails managing and mitigating vulnerabilities continuously to reduce an organization's overall security risks. In comparison, Security Architecture is looking at security as a whole across an entire organization and developing strategies to improve and become more efficient from a security standpoint. While working in a casino was eye-opening, I wanted a bigger challenge and decided to move to the vendor side of security. I am currently a Sales Engineer on the technical side of sales for one of the largest tech and security vendors in the world. Go figure!

One thing about me, I love projects. I like to build things that have meaning and are useful for my customers. Understanding this about myself helped me to understand my "WHY" better. My "WHY" is to create a space for women and minorities to be successful in cyber. Whether that is through my sales role, selling security automation tools; or through Cyberjutsu, the nonprofit I run that seeks to empower women to network and lead in cyber, if I can help just one person see their potential, I have done my job.

Let's talk about Cyberjutsu for a minute. This organization is near and dear to my heart, as it is a nonprofit cyber community of women, girls, allies, and all those in between working, growing, and learning about cyber *together*. We provide affordable hands-on training and networking opportunities to help women enter and advance in cyberspace. It's a safe space to learn and build, and we want our members to find their #cyberjutsutribe and excel in the cyber industry, and I want to help you do the same.

Over the course of my career, I have had numerous mentors, both male and female, allies and friends, teach me things you typically only learn from experience. My network has helped shape me into the professional I am today. Those experiences have led me to develop what I call my *Cyber Cycle of Success*. Whenever the time comes for a change or move, I implement the ideas of leading with a "you first" mentality, securing my people power, and maintaining my skills and relationships. This is a continuous process, and I want to help you create your own cyber cycle of success. We will walk through the three pillars that I have used to gain success in my career. While you want to start by taking initiative, taking initiative is intertwined with the entire process. So let's start there. Initiative, in its basic form, means "the power or ability to begin or to follow through energetically with a plan or task."

Leading With a "You First" Mentality

I know that sounds a little selfish, but hear me out. Cyber can be brutal, but it can also be rewarding. In my LinkedIn Learning course, "Landing Your First Cybersecurity Job", I introduce you to the PIVOT framework from my good friend Victor Malloy. This framework allows you to develop your action plan and start the cycle for success. Let's break down each letter:

Pause: Develop and understand "WHY" you want to enter cyber. Understanding this helps you create a plan based on that "WHY." It also gives you something to refer back to when things get tough.

Inventory: You probably already have many skills that can be used in cyber, so let's inventory those. Let's say you are a teacher. You have presentation skills, organizational skills, curriculum development experience, research and development skills, and probably a list of other things. These skills can translate to a position such as being a trainer or developer of a cyber curriculum. During this stage, it is also good to list skills you would like to obtain. This can help make the job search a little easier.

Vision: What is your vision for your future in cyber? What do you want to accomplish in this space? What type of impact do you want to make? This can change as you move through your career, which is okay. Identify it and *write it down*. My vision is to help change the face of cyber by helping to equip women and minorities with the skills and tools needed to be successful.

Organize: Now, it's time to organize a plan of action toward success. This part may seem a little difficult at first, but this is your opportunity to start researching the field of cyber if you haven't already begun that process. What type of work do you want to do? What roles have you seen that may interest you? Who are the people to follow and potentially add to your network? What cyber resources are you currently using to gain skills? If there are no answers to these, create a plan to do the research.

Take action: This is probably one of the most important parts of this framework: taking action. It means nothing if you do all the work to understand your *why*, inventory your skills, create a vision, and get organized if you don't take the initiative to *act* on what you have done. You have put a great amount of time and effort into getting to this point, and that shouldn't go to waste. So, take the initiative to take action and execute your plan.

Cyber isn't a place to sit and wait for things to happen. No one will hold your hand every step of the way. You, as the individual badass that you are, have to take that first step of leading with a "you first" mentality. The PIVOT framework allows you to gain clarity about your goals and understand where you need a little more assistance and support. Take the initiative to research and reach out to people to start growing your network and your net worth.

This leads to the second idea of Securing Your People Power, your network.

Securing Your People Power

When I first started in tech, I hated the role I was in. I was the only woman and Black person on my team, and it sucked. I felt alone because there weren't many people with my background who I could bounce ideas off or go to for advice. This forced me to think bigger and look outside of my company for support. I had to start thinking about my network and securing my people power.

Networking is huge in cyber. The majority of the roles that I have held have come from people in my network who know my skill set and vocalize that to hiring teams and leaders. This is how I got my foot in the door, and you can too. I have an advisory team of people in and outside of cyber that I can call on to discuss ideas, challenges, and successes. Your advisory team should consist of five to six people who you can reach out to when needed and know that they will provide the necessary support. Your advisory team supplements your strengths and experiences with their own.

My advisory team consists of a:

Cheerleader: Someone who can cheer you on and uplift your spirits. They are rooting for you to be successful. They can be from a completely different industry or even from your family.

Mentor: Someone with more experience in specific areas who can provide valuable professional insight.

These people can be your sounding board for specific issues or concerns.

Sponsor: Similar to a cheerleader, but this person puts your name up for consideration and advocates for you in rooms and spaces you are not in. You may have these people in your circle already.

Connector: This person helps to connect you to resources and people to further your success in the space.

Constructive Trustee: This person will provide honest, constructive feedback on your activities and goals. The truth can sometimes hurt, so finding someone who knows how to give it to you straight without making you feel less than others is important.

Consider some of these questions when building your team: Who sharpens me? Who stretches my thinking? Who is willing to provide constructive feedback? Who brings new perspectives and ideas to my life?

Make sure when you ask people to join your advisory team; you have an elevator pitch ready that includes how much time you have as well as what stage of your career you are in. And remember, as your career progresses, your advisory team members may change, and people may say "No." That is okay. By then, your network will have grown, and you can select new people to join the team.

In addition to your advisory board, you should also network with the larger cyber community. By joining organizations like the Women's Society of Cyberjutsu (Cyberjutsu), Black Girls Hack, Black Girls In Cyber, Minorities in Cyber, and others, you get instant access to a worldwide network. At Cyberjutsu, we call this network, this community, the #cyberjutsutribe, filled with cheerleaders, mentors, sponsors, and more who can help you navigate cyberspace.

LinkedIn is also a great place to start building your network. Look for folks with similar skill sets or in roles you are interested in and reach out to them. Let them know who you are and what you are hoping to accomplish and contribute to the connection that is being made. Engage with their posts with meaningful content; don't just say "I agree" to something they posted. Be intentional in what you are communicating. Those coming behind you will look to you for guidance as well!

Cyberjutsu gave me a community. My advisory team has given me access to opportunities for learning, leadership, and employment. Because of them, I can give back to others through mentorship, speaking, and community-building. This allows me to expand my reach to more people. Giving back is just as important as building your team and taking initiative. When you have learned something, you have something to share.

Maintenance is Key

You've established a strong foundation by taking the initiative to understand the cyber industry better, thought about who your advisory team should be, and are growing your network. Now, it's time to maintain the skills and relationships you have created. This isn't a "set it and forget it" strategy. If you do that, they will forget you.

Maintenance is a continuous cycle throughout your career, no matter your industry. This can include training and education in various formats, leadership and technical training, writing blogs and books about your skills and experiences, and speaking at conferences and events to share your knowledge. These are a few ways to continue to hone your skills. This also leads to growing your brand and reach both within and outside your organization.

Reach out to your advisory team and let them know what you are working on, what challenges you are having, and the accomplishments you have achieved. This can be via email, phone call, or meeting for happy hour. Whatever works best, just stay in contact. I like to check in with my folks every few weeks and sometimes more often if something is pressing and I need assistance with.

I remember when I first found Cyberjutsu in 2013, I had just failed my ISC2 Certified Information Systems Security Professional (CISSP) certification exam. I was looking for a study group to help me achieve it. At that point, I didn't have a brand, and I wasn't the face of anything. Joining Cyberjutsu changed that. I now had a platform to share my knowledge and experience. That's when I launched my brand. This allowed me to start thinking bigger as it pertained to my career and what I wanted to do over the next few decades.

Maintaining your skills and relationships isn't the only maintenance you should consider. You also have to maintain YOU: your mind, your space, and your peace. As you take this journey into cyber, self-care is so important. I mentioned earlier that this industry can wear you out. Cyberjutsu gave me a way to practice self-care. Maintaining yourself is just as important as maintaining your skills and relationships. You can't be your best self if you don't take care of yourself. When caring for YOU, you give your mind, body, and spirit permission to relax and be still. You have the time to reflect and release the stresses you may have encountered.

I like to meditate, build Legos, and get my nails done. During these times, my mind is free to explore possibilities. It gives me space to find solutions to challenges I may have in my personal and professional life.

How you practice self-care is completely up to you. Find spaces and activities that allow you to focus on yourself and relax. Give your mind a break. You will be grateful in the long run.

Your time is now. So, as you start down this path of exploring cyber, think about how you want to walk this journey. It's time to define your Cyber Cycle of Success.

Write it down! A visual reminder of where you want to go helps you stay on track. Get a piece of paper and start with your "why" at the top of the page. Think of this as a wheel with you in the center; your strengths, weaknesses, needs, and wants are the spokes of the inner circle. Write down high-level milestones that you want to reach and what success looks like for each one. From there think about the people, advisory team, and network that can help you at each of those spokes to reach the next level. Because this is a wheel there will be cyclical development in each area and that is just what you want. As you build your skills some of your weaknesses will start to become strengths. New weaknesses may develop as you move into different roles that will require learning new things. Needs may become wants and vice versa. You have a plan and can adjust accordingly.

You are the creator of your future, and these steps should help you get clear on what that can look like as you pedal forward.

Mari Galloway

Chief Executive Officer | Cyberjutsu

Mari is the CEO and a founding board member for the Women's Society of Cyberjutsu (WSC), one of the fastest growing 501(c)3 non-profit cyber communities dedicated to bringing more women and girls to cyber. WSC provides its members with the resources and support required to enter and advance as cyber professionals.

Mari began her career with Accenture where she excelled as a Network Engineer. Mari is also the inaugural ISC2 Diversity Award winner for 2019. With over 14 years in Information Technology, 12 of which are in cyber. Her experience spans network design and security architecture, risk assessments, vulnerability management, incident response, and policy development across government and commercial industries.

She holds a variety of technical and management certifications (CISSP, GIAC, CCNA, to name a few) as well as a Bachelor's degree in Computer Information Systems from Columbus State University and a Master of Science in Information Systems from Strayer University. Mari is also a published author and a LinkedIn Learning author.

Mari is currently a resident of Las Vegas and is the CEO of a thriving bookkeeping and cyber consulting business. She is a published author and regularly contributes content to security blogs and training companies across the country as well as an Adjunct Professor for UMGC and LinkedIn Learning instructor. She also lends her time to various organizations as an award judge, mentor, and advisor. Outside of being a geek, Mari enjoys arts, puzzles, and Legos!

Linkedin: https://www.linkedin.com/in/themarigalloway

Website: www.themarigalloway.com

CHAPTER 6

Cyber Power - How I Leveraged My Cyber Career to Break the Poverty Pipeline

By: Carla Plummer

"The most radical act of combating generational poverty is to learn new ways to leverage your brilliance, gifts, talents, and skills in ways that generate profit despite the societal and economic limitations; it's a measure of challenging the norm and daring to believe big and do things differently"

I am a product of my environment. Growing up, my environment was not a reflection of the American Dream that celebrated the acquisition of wealth. There were no lavish homes, perfectly manicured lawns, or white picket fences in my community. I would never have imagined that being a "product of my environment" would become an asset along my career journey. What once seemed like a limitation has now become the very thing that incites purpose and fuels my passion to change the narrative that being a product of where you come from is inherently negative, when in fact, it is a pillar of resilience and a beacon of inspiration.

My story began in sunny South Florida. Most South Florida natives believe that if you can survive the southernmost parts of the Sunshine State, then you are innately and adequately prepared to survive anywhere in the world. But I imagine that these sentiments ring true for anyone who grew up in a tough environment and has had to endure challenges to survive and thrive in a society where their access to resources was limited and often scarce. When we think of the statistical perspective and stereotypical dynamics that accommodate being raised below the poverty line, my upbringing was a reflection of the societal expectations that many would assume to be present and prevalent. My father was a drug dealer and spent most of my adolescent years incarcerated. My mother, who became a teen mom to my oldest sister at the tender age of thirteen, made ends meet for my sisters and me the best way that she could as a single mom of three. My family pedigree did not include anyone that was college educated and very few of my family members had even received a high school diploma. Determined to not repeat the cycle of generational poverty, I made a conscious decision to pursue excellence and the financial security that eluded my family during my formative years.

Against all odds, I became the first person in my family to graduate college and I eventually landed a rewarding and well-paid career in cyber. The journey was not easy. As a kid, I pored over university catalogs, determined to attend college. My mom was always the biggest supporter of my dreams, often doing whatever she could within her means to support my growth. However, even with that, it was hard getting out of the generational cycle of familiar habits. From the day we were born, we were placed in the same box our families have lived in for generations before us, unable to see the very stars we strive to reach for. Within that box, we learned to assimilate. We became owners of fears and burdens that were not originally ours. Along the way, we grew fearful of breaking the mold or outgrowing others. We became apprehensive to venture outside of the box because of the fear of some imperial hand looming above seeking to pluck us up and shove us right back in our place at any moment. Many of us suffer the worst kind of fear when those in the box with us who share in our despair would intentionally pull us back in. Without great advocacy, this box becomes the mental trap that has plagued so many of us. My purpose is to guide you through a few lessons that I learned as I ventured beyond the mental and societal constraints of generational poverty and into a rewarding career in cyber.

Lesson #1: Establishing the Vision

When establishing the vision for your career, my recommendation is to keep it simple, remain flexible, and never subject yourself to stringent deadlines. Don't get me wrong, deadlines can be a good motivator but always weigh the possible vs. the probable. Your vision should have a main objective and then milestones outlined on how you plan to reach that objective. Your vision should ground you and recenter your focus. Your vision should also change as you change and life changes. It's ok to scratch the first, second, or even third versions of your vision as you gain experiences. In this age of social media, it is very easy to get caught up in what others are doing and how much they have achieved in comparison to you. On top of that, for those of us who finally worked up enough courage to step out of our generational box, there is an excessive amount of pressure to succeed, to be the first. At times you may feel like it would be easier to just go back and be with everyone else. That is a mental mirage, whether we stay in the generational cycle of familiar habits or venture out of the box, there will be challenges. We are merely choosing which set of challenges we will accept. The vision will serve as your roadmap. Always remember that just because something doesn't happen by a certain time frame does not mean you shouldn't still go after it.

Lesson #2: Understanding your value

Society has a way of placing labels on people. They tell us who we are and what we will become before we've even had the opportunity to make those self-discoveries on our own. As you embark upon this journey you have to know and understand the value you bring to the table. If you are like me, our upbringing has given us a specific set of skills that, if used correctly, can be very valuable to a career in cyber. Being a product of your environment is not a bad thing. There will be a measure of unlearning and habit-breaking you will need to undergo as part of this journey, but that does not mean you have to become someone that you are not or abandon the core skills that you developed as a result of your environment. I didn't understand my superpowers at the beginning of my journey, but I do now. My mental fortitude is a direct result of my environment and upbringing. Here are a few other skills that come naturally to people who grew up like me:

- Tact

- Problem-solving

- Resiliency

- Resourcefulness

- Discernment

Don't be shy to showcase your strengths and what sets you apart. In this industry, it's a must.

Lesson #3: Handle setbacks strategically

Let's face it, things do not always go as planned. Life can simply get the best of us at times. Do not confuse a setback with failure and then ultimately a reason to run back into the familiarity of "the box". I'm sure there is someone back in that box who you could run to and who would coddle you like no other. But rest assured, you don't need to be spared the disappointments. The fact that you even dared to venture outside of the box tells me that you have a special dose of grit and determination. You must believe that about yourself. Retreating to the cyclical habits of normal, familiar, and expected will only lead to unsurmountable feelings of regret. Instead, when you face a situation that may cause you delays in achieving a milestone, think about what you gained from it. What you look for, you will find; let's condition ourselves to look for the positives. Those positives can catapult you if you tap into them.

Part of how I ended up on a career path that would eventually lead to being a Security Engineer for multiple Fortune 500 companies was due to what I perceived as a failure at the time. When I graduated with my Bachelor's Degree in Electrical Engineering, I had neither job prospects nor a plan in the middle of a recession. I made the decision to go back home feeling like a complete failure. Then one day, out of the blue, my old work-study boss called and asked me if I would be interested in being his back-fill because he was leaving the university and he knew I was looking for work. This wasn't an esteemed position with

"Engineer's pay" like I thought I would get after graduating, and I almost let my ego get in the way because of what I thought I was due after going through such a rigorous curriculum and obtaining my degree. However, looking back at it now, that position was a very necessary stop on my journey. It was my catapult.

Lesson #4: Reputation, consistency, and accountability

In this industry your reputation is everything and, on this journey, your level of success will be directly tied to your consistency. You have to take accountability very seriously and root out all inconsistency that's within you. I once heard the motivational speaker Inky Johnson say, "How you do anything is how you will do everything." Even the smallest task will require the same amount of consistency as the largest one. I told you the story of how I obtained my very first opportunity after graduating college. Had it not been for a few key relationships that I cultivated when I was a work-study student, my name would not have been mentioned for the opportunity, especially since it was not a job that I had applied for or even knew existed. I like to call these types of key relationships "champions." I've had many people I'd consider a champion throughout my journey. Your champion will oftentimes ruffle a few feathers for you, recommend you for opportunities, ensure that you get the raise you deserve, and advocate for you with the sole intent to expand your reach. This type of advocacy does not come easy. To get someone in your corner like this, you will need to get out of your comfort zone and network but most importantly you need to develop a track record. Your track record is developed by consistently showing up and doing what you said you were going to do, at a noteworthy quality. The "Golden Rule" in my house that I was held accountable to was to finish everything that I started, even after the initial motivation had faded. People are always watching. No one will be willing to put their name and reputation on the line for someone inconsistent and fair-weathered.

✦ Your Call to Action:

Take some time to research potential cyber career paths you would like to explore. From there look up people in similar roles and job postings for those types of roles to build your milestones lists of credentials you need to achieve as part of your overall vision. Remember that you already possess certain skills that should not be discounted.

Do a skills assessment as part of establishing your vision. Think specifically about life experiences as well as other jobs you've had and the skills you've gained because of those experiences. Many transferable skills get overlooked because people assume that just because they were not tied to a specific job, it does not count. Remember that it all counts, you just need to understand what they are and how to apply them in different arenas. Lastly, I want you to do a self-assessment. I mentioned in Lesson #4 that you will need to hold yourself accountable for being inconsistent. That's going to require you to be honest with yourself. This does not mean beating yourself up for dropping the ball, but instead being honest and acknowledging that you did drop the ball instead of passing the blame off on someone else and then working toward corrective actions.

Let your resilience be the guiding light on your journey to success in the cyber world. Embrace your unique background, value your strengths, and stay focused on your vision. Together, we can change the narrative and inspire others to break free from the shackles of their past.

Carla Plummer

Senior Information Security Engineer

Carla is an accomplished engineer with an extensive track record spanning over 12 years in IT and Information Security. Carla stands as a trailblazer as a first-generation college graduate. She holds a Bachelor of Science degree in Electrical Engineering and a Master of Science in Cybersecurity, both proudly earned at the University of South Florida. Moreover, her commitment to excellence is underscored by her possession of several industry-recognized certifications.

Carla has had the honor of serving as the Co-Director of the Cybersecurity Curriculum at Black Girls in Cyber (BGiC), a prominent non-profit organization. She is a proud member of Zeta Phi Beta Sorority, Incorporated, and a staunch advocate for diversity and inclusion within the realm of Cyber. She ardently believes that a career in this field is accessible to individuals from all walks of life. Her overarching mission is to empower women with similar backgrounds, encouraging them to tap into their innate creativity and potential. In doing so, she aspires to shed light on the myriad opportunities awaiting discovery within this captivating and ever-evolving field.

Beyond her professional accolades, Carla is a devoted wife to her husband, Johnathan, and a caring mother to two young boys, Cameron & Jacob.

Linkedin:
https://www.linkedin.com/in/carla-plummer-8164651a/

CHAPTER 7

The Corporate Athlete:
Learn the Game, Play the Game, Change the Game

By: Tia Hopkins

"Confidence has no competition."

From the time we're born, far too many women of color see our growth potential stunted, and our curiosity discouraged. We encounter glass ceilings and, often, are denied one of the most basic human rights — the freedom to find and be oneself. Rather than letting us become who we are, we're told who we should be, what we should love, how we should carry ourselves, and sadly, in many cases, which career to pursue. For women of color, a career path in cyber isn't often presented as viable or realistic. And it's not because we don't have the potential to fall in love with or excel in the field, it's most often due to a lack of awareness, exposure, representation, and overall confidence in our ability to be successful.

Directive guidance often bestowed upon Black children from our childhood such as "keep your head down", "don't make a fuss", "do as you're told", "always be polite", "smile and nod", and "don't talk back" were meant to keep us safe in a society where something as simple as the color of our skin could be perceived as threatening, or used as an excuse for unfair treatment. Although these types of directive guidance were meant to protect us, they have had unintended consequences on our psyche as we move into adulthood and become working professionals. As a result, building political capital in the workplace and taking up space in rooms where you are the only Black woman becomes a psychological feat.

Things like imposter syndrome become a normal state of mind. Wondering whether we belong, and doubts about our personal paths and choices are common among women of color in all industries, but especially in cyber where we make up a very small percentage of the workforce. Although imposter syndrome isn't isolated to Black women, it is exacerbated for us due to gender, race, and cultural beliefs and disparities.

The challenges I've faced throughout my professional journey were significantly compounded by the fact that I am an introverted southern Black woman, neurodiverse lesbian, and 4-time college dropout. I was raised by a single mother (the most amazing mother a girl could ask for), bullied in school, and I am a survivor of low self-confidence, constant microaggressions, homelessness, and abuse. I struggled to find my place in this world - let alone in this industry. One day I decided that I'd had enough. I was done apologizing for who I am and feeling like my existence was a disruption to the daily lives of others.

The more I remained true to myself, the more I began to build confidence. This also gave the world the opportunity to accept me for who I am, instead of who I pretended to be. This shift allowed me to see that although I may not be a fit everywhere, I am a fit somewhere - and I am okay with that. I didn't know it back then, but my struggles were shaping me into who I am today and developing my superpowers: overcoming adversity, being comfortable with being uncomfortable, not seeking validation, and being hellbent on using my setbacks and lessons learned to help others move forward.

I began my career as a high-speed internet installer with the local phone company – DSL (Digital Subscriber Line) Installer to be specific. Telecommunications and internet connectivity was my primary focus, but I was curious about the networking and computing aspects, even though it was not my responsibility. Connecting multiple computers, enabling wireless connectivity, and configuring firewalls for online safety were topics I was asked for guidance on regularly, but I did not have the knowledge or training required to assist in these areas.

Back then, I did not have a mentor or any type of career guidance, could not afford certifications, and had a handful of false starts in college for various reasons. Despite all of this, I was determined to be successful, so I searched for examples of what success looked like in my peers and leaders so I could *learn* more about myself, potential career opportunities, and any perceived gaps in education and experience I should be aware of.

About a year into my role as a DSL installer, I had my *'level-up'* plan figured out. I was able to save enough money to purchase a few computers, a router, and a switch from the local thrift store, and eventually built my first home lab. I even splurged a bit and purchased two books to help guide me along the way: *Computers for Dummies* and *Networking for Dummies*. My roommate thought I was insane, but I was so proud. I practiced and studied for months, and after gaining some confidence, I decided it was time to *play*, or apply what I'd learned in the real world. I began answering questions from customers that I'd been unable to answer previously. This created opportunities for me to provide IT services to businesses and homeowners and earn extra money. This was the catalyst for my professional growth and, unbeknownst to me, where my life began to *change*.

After many years with the phone company, I wanted more for my career, so I decided to pursue a full-time role in IT. Breaking into the industry proved to be extremely difficult. There I was, trying to pursue a career in a white male-dominated industry as a young, Black, tattooed, and masculine-of-center woman. Not to mention, I had no industry certifications, no degree, and no professional network, but again, I was determined to be successful.

I submitted applications for what felt like hundreds of jobs, the majority of which seemed to just go into a black hole. The interviews I was lucky enough to land were strange at best. The conversations felt like the decision was made to not hire me as soon as I walked in the door. Instead of being asked to speak about the experience I did have, I was mostly torn down for the experience I didn't have. No one was interested in my aptitude for learning, my curiosity, or my grit.

There were days I questioned whether I'd ever have an opportunity to prove myself. There were times when things just felt too hard and seemed unfair; I wanted to quit. Instead of giving up, I continued to remind myself of who I am and the value I bring. I remember looking in the mirror and coaching myself, saying things like, "The right leader at the right company will see your potential, and you will have your shot." I told myself if I ever landed a role in IT, I'd make sure the company that gave me a chance knew it was the best decision they'd ever made; and that one day, I'd make sure the naysayers and those who rejected me could see what they missed out on by being shortsighted.

And then it happened – someone took a chance on me. I accepted a role as a network and systems administrator. I worked hard. I was resourceful. I went above and beyond and exceeded expectations. The role was only supposed to be part-time, but after only two weeks on the job, I was offered a full-time position. Within two years, still with no degree and now one certification (CompTIA A+), I'd found my way to an IT Director position at a NY-based company where I worked directly with the CEO to transform his break/fix retail shop into a successful managed services business.

Prior to becoming an IT Director, I was heads down and on the grind. I said yes to every opportunity and stepped up for every challenge - whether I felt like I was ready or not. I believed in myself, and I was confident that my grit, resourcefulness, relentless drive, and curiosity would carry me while I continued to learn and grow. I carried this attitude with me for the first couple of years in my director role, then imposter syndrome started to creep in. I remember reviewing job descriptions for director-level positions in IT and feeling like a fraud. I was doing the job, sure, but I still did not have a post-secondary education or degree, nor did I have advanced certifications. Unfortunately, based on my research and feedback from recruiters, I felt like that was part of the game - that those pieces of paper mattered more than what I'd actually accomplished in my career. In fact, it appeared that I would never have the opportunity to discuss my achievements with a prospective employer because my lack of formal education was seen as a barrier to entry - I wasn't good enough on paper to be viewed as a viable candidate.

I began to question what was next for me. I'd gone from feeling great about my ability to navigate on my own and make it this far, to feeling stuck and uncertain about the future. I had to be honest with myself and acknowledge the fact that I really needed to figure out my next move because grit and grind would only take me so far. I realized that my previous goals had gone from out of reach to obtained, my work environment had gone from predictable to uncertain, and my career trajectory had gone from exciting to stagnant. I needed to play a different game to change my circumstances - it was time for a new level-up plan.

I decided to go back to school to pursue a B.S. in Information Technology. I had every reason in the world to believe this journey would end up as dropout number five, but I challenged myself and I promised myself this time would be different. It was tough, and there were times I wanted to quit, but I held myself accountable. When I graduated, I was the first person in my family to receive a college degree. I can't begin to describe the overwhelming sense of accomplishment I felt after achieving a goal that seemed so far out of reach. From that moment on, I was unstoppable. As the saying goes, success can be addictive.

While working towards my bachelor's degree, I noticed a shift in the job market. Job descriptions seemed to target more specialized skills. Whereas "jack of all trades" was previously viewed as a differentiation, "master of none" was increasingly becoming the underlying designation. At the time, the skills that appeared to be most in demand were software development, cloud, and cybersecurity. The more I researched, the more cybersecurity spoke to me, so I earned an M.S. in Computer and Information Systems Security and Assurance, and a second M.S. in Cybersecurity and Information Assurance immediately following my bachelor's degree. While in pursuit of those degrees, I also obtained several industry certifications including CISSP, C|EH, ITIL, and Security+. I often joke about the fact that my career is my hobby, but it's true; cybersecurity is my true passion. Many years ago, I chose cybersecurity as my 'thing', it chose me back, and we've been choosing each other ever since.

Cybersecurity was a function of my role as IT Director, but I wanted it to be the focus of my career. I firmly believed my success in IT thus far was largely due to my hands-on skills and I was convinced that transitioning to cybersecurity in a leadership role would narrow my real-world experience and dilute my value. I would later learn that this was not the case, but for better or worse, I left my role as IT Director for a role as a Security Systems Engineer.

Very early into my new role, I started asking questions; lots of them. I needed to *learn* and understand what was expected of me, what good looked like, and find some shining examples of people labeled as industry rock stars so I could figure out how to make an impact. It was important to me to understand what I was responsible for and how to crush it in my role before I did anything else. What I quickly learned was that I was at risk. I did not have a security-focused seller in my territory, which meant I would only be brought in on projects if resources in other territories were overutilized - I was an underutilized resource. In business, value comes in many forms. It was clear that financial value was at the top of the list, but my ability to drive financial value was out of my control, so I had to find a way to show value that was within my control. I had to figure out a way to *play* the game to my advantage, so I could *change* my situation.

I began building relationships and learning more about the business. I followed my previous playbook of saying yes to everything and volunteering to step in and help in situations that were outside my comfort zone. I noticed a pattern beginning to develop: I was able to show the most value in areas of the business that had the least amount of support– areas of the business that were still being developed, vendor certifications that were needed but had not been pursued by other engineers, and a lack of subject matter expertise in emerging technologies and markets. It also occurred to me that the opportunity for my role as a DSL installer came about for a similar reason: very few of the seasoned telecommunications technicians were interested in this new endeavor– it was too new, too uncertain. This epiphany brought me to my career philosophy, which is instead of competing in the oversaturated areas of the business and market, go make an impact in the emerging areas that aren't saturated.

Six months into my role as Security Systems Engineer, I was promoted to Security Solutions Architect, the role that was previously vacant, leaving the Security Systems Engineer at risk. I was now a double-edged sword, heavily entrenched in the business, and having a meaningful impact on company revenue and customer relationships. I was comfortable again. My work environment had gone from uncertain to predictable and my career trajectory had gone from at risk to full of opportunity. Suddenly, for the first time in my career, recruiters were knocking on *my* door. I was content in my role and learning a lot, which was my goal at the time, so I didn't respond to many of the requests until one day an opportunity came along that really piqued my interest and aligned with my career philosophy.

My next move was to a rapidly growing startup in a disruptive space in the cybersecurity industry. A huge risk, yes, but full of endless opportunities. I joined the company at the individual contributor level and rose to C-level executive after being promoted 5 times since beginning my career with the company - nearly once per year. I'm often asked how I was able to navigate in a way that allowed me to differentiate myself from my peers and accelerate my career advancement. I simply followed my playbook: *Learn the Game, Play the Game, Change the Game*. Only this time, the changes impacted more than me and my situation - they impacted an entire industry.

I originally joined the company as a Solutions Architect; very similar to my previous role. I consulted and advised C-level technology leaders and offered guidance as to how my company's solutions could help them address their security challenges. I absolutely loved my job. I was part of an amazing team, worked with great people, and benefitted from incredible leadership. But still, it's a new game with new rules, and by this time, I've learned from many successes and failures in my career, so I trust my playbook a lot more and I'm following it to the letter: learn the game, play the game, change the game. I first focus on myself and my role/team, then branch out to other teams within the organization to get to know people and build relationships, and finally, stretch myself to learn more about the business.

A little over a year into my new role, I was promoted to Team Lead. This promotion brought on additional responsibilities such as mentoring other members of the team and collaborating cross-functionally to improve customer outcomes. I was already doing this as part of my normal day-to-day, so it didn't feel much like a change in scope. I was still comfortable. Little by little, however, I noticed an uptick in requests for assistance with special projects, speaking engagements, and complex opportunities. I wasn't sure why my assistance was being requested over the other talented individuals on the team, but I took it as an opportunity and rose to meet the challenge.

I had no goal in mind other than being the best I could be for myself, my team, and my company, and continuing to build relationships and learn more about the business. Less than six months after being promoted to Team Lead, I was presented with an opportunity that should have been exciting, but it was absolutely terrifying.

An opening for the VP of Global Solutions Architecture had become available and I was encouraged to apply. This meant that I would be leading the entire team of individuals who were my peers at the time. I was frustrated. I was perfectly fine where I was, doing what I was doing. Every thought I had in response was negative; all laced with imposter syndrome. "I've been a leader before, but not like this." "Why do they want me for this role, what makes them think I'd be good at it?" "There are so many other qualified individuals on the team." and the list goes on and on. But then I had to snap myself out of it. I had to, as I like to say, *rebuke imposter syndrome* and strip it of its power. Instead of coming up with a list of reasons why I wouldn't be successful, I came up with one reason that I would be - because I'm me.

I had no idea how much this moment would *change* my life. I applied for the role and after a number of interviews, I got the job. Now, my team is literally *my* team, and instead of supporting their ability to be successful, I'm responsible for their success. I led an entire team of industry professionals older than me, some more seasoned than me, and none who looked like me; a few of them having unsuccessfully applied for the role I was currently in - all of whom just days prior had been my equals. There were undertones of tokenism and favoritism; there were even some expressions of disbelief, attitudes of insubordination, and numerous statements made with, "we'll see" as the underlying sentiment. I could write an entire book on what the journey from team lead to vice president was like, and one day I might, but a few of the key things that helped me during my transition were the relationships I built, being transparent and unafraid to ask questions or seek guidance, and meeting people where they are. Of course, we are now back to a new game with new rules, but what's different about this time - and it took me a while to realize it, and a bit longer to accept it - is that the game and the rules are mine to shape. So not only am I able to learn the game and play it to my advantage, I'm able to change the game to my advantage and to the advantage of others as well - now I have influence.

Since then, I have been promoted several times and taken on additional responsibilities that have stretched me and shown me things about myself that I never knew existed. Over the years, I have transitioned from working *in* the business as an individual contributor and vice president to working *on* the business as a C-level executive, where I am able to combine my knowledge as a cybersecurity practitioner with my knowledge of the industry to achieve corporate goals and drive enterprise value. These opportunities have been presented to me as a result of my thought leadership, problem-solving capabilities, and constant pursuit of differentiation in the market - both for myself and my company. I have most recently earned my place in the corporate boardroom where I will continue to learn and identify opportunities for growth and change.

I have now branded myself *The Cyber Equalizer*™ because I am incredibly passionate about making cybersecurity accessible to everyone whether advising corporate board directors and senior executives or shaping the minds of industry newcomers. I took the long road by going down the IT generalist path before focusing on cybersecurity, but my journey has made me wiser, so I wouldn't change a thing. For those coming after me, however, the road doesn't have to be nearly as difficult. Despite life's many challenges, I remained dedicated and steadfast in my pursuits and am now at a point in my career as an industry influencer and thought leader where I believe my story and my experiences can help others navigate their own journeys with confidence.

As part of my personal journey, I played women's tackle football for twelve years; I currently coach an international women's team – football changed and, quite frankly, saved my life. My confidence, team player mentality, work ethic, and even my leadership style have been influenced by things I learned (and continue to learn) on and off the field. Football's greatest gift to me, however, is my philosophy – Learn the Game, Play the Game, Change the Game, which has served me very well in the advancement of my career. I encourage you to learn, play, and change the game every day in your own life, and here I've shared a few plays from the playbooks in my upcoming book to help you get started.

Learn the game.

Each phase brings its own unique challenges, of course, but for me, the learning stage was the most challenging initially. The reason for this is that learning doesn't begin with industry knowledge, degrees, or technical certifications. It begins with you. It begins with knowing yourself – yes, knowing your worth, what you bring to the table, and your non-negotiables, but also leaning into the areas where you're not so great – your knowledge and experience gaps, your fears, your triggers, your biases. We all have them, and this self-discovery process takes a great deal of honesty, self-awareness, and emotional intelligence. But doing the work brings with it a heightened sense of who you are and what you represent, which will go a long way in improving your professional interactions.

You also need to learn your environment – whether personal or professional. And by that, I mean you need to learn and understand how the game is played and who the other players are, so you're prepared when it's time to play. The way you show up can help or hurt your chances of success, so be mindful of this throughout your journey and always come back to it; this is a continuous process.

Additionally, build a team of players around you (advocates, sponsors, peers, mentors, coaches, etc.) that can help you win – think of this team as your personal advisory board. As you're learning, share with the team and develop game-winning strategies together. You are the star of your team, and everyone has an important position to play. You want to make sure you're doing your best to set the team up for success.

Running the Play:

- Be self-aware and emotionally intelligent.
- Always be honest with yourself and true to yourself.
- Don't believe everything you think.
- Don't be afraid to ask hard questions.
- Be relentlessly curious.

Play the game.

Learning doesn't stop here. Playing is essentially applying what you've learned. At this stage, you're feeling things out, gaining confidence, establishing credibility, networking and building relationships, etc. - all the things that tee you up to change the game. Playing is where the grind begins, and it can be scary. It's the time when you suit up and go play ball, and without a doubt, you're going to see and experience some things you never have before. A coach once said to me, "Football doesn't build character, it reveals it." He was right. Football, much like our careers, shows us who we are, and we get to decide who we want to be. When you get knocked down, will you bounce back and get up? How will you apply what you've learned? How are you going to respond when things don't go your way? More importantly, how will you react when things go well for you? Being emotionally balanced is important - never get too high or too low.

One day I was at football practice and I was frustrated because I wasn't doing well in one of our drills. I tried over and over again. Finally, something clicked and I nailed it. I was beside myself with excitement. I immediately looked over at my coach for approval, a pat on the back, anything. He looked at me with the straightest face I've ever seen and said, "Don't just do it till you get it right, do it till you can't get it wrong." I was less than pleased with him at the time, of course, but he was right. I carried that mentality with me beyond my football career and into my professional career; it changed my life.

I share this story with you because when you're on the path to greatness, good enough is never good enough - you need to be great. Said another way, if you want to change the game, the way you need to play comes down to adding value, getting sticky, and gaining influence.

1. **Add Value** - there's a difference between doing your job and being a valuable asset to your team. When you interview for a role, you're given a description of what the expectations are. If you were to do those things and

do them well every single day, you'd probably be fine, but you want more than that. Right?

2. **Get Sticky** - this means you've found a way to leave a mark that would have a significant negative impact on the company or team if you were to leave. Whether it's something you do, something you know, or just the way you do something, no one does it quite like you. And sure, if you left, business would go on as business does, but it just wouldn't be the same without you. Dare I say there would be a bit of a setback?

3. **Gain Influence** - you can't make change without influence. A person of influence is defined as someone having the ability to affect change in an indirect, but typically important fashion. You want to be in the room or called into the room when important decisions are made. You want your leaders and peers to seek and value your feedback and perspective because once you have their ears, they're listening to your voice.

Running the Play:

- Master the art of disarming (meet people where they are, then show them who you are).
- Be a disruptor without being disruptive.

- Go hard or go home.

- Be unforgettable and irreplaceable.

- Earn a seat at the table. The *table* is an intimate gathering, not a family cookout, so seating is limited. This won't be easy.

Change the game.

Once you've built a brand and people are saying your name when you're not in the room, you're ready to affect change. People are now listening to you, following you, and looking for you. As you're becoming more and more of a change-maker, it's important to bring people along with you, share your success, and lift as you climb. Learning and playing the game is great and all, but when you can help someone else be great as well, you've officially arrived as a change agent. Not many people wake up in the morning and say, "I'm gonna change some lives today!" But those of us that do are changing the world one person at a time. This much-needed change in the cybersecurity industry is what motivates me to put myself in more unfamiliar situations and play games that maybe weren't even on my list of games to play. I do it because I believe it is my responsibility to be the change I want to see - and what I want to see is more people who look like me in the room and at the table with me. Finally, I will leave you with a personal quote of mine – 'Being smart gets you noticed, being informed keeps you relevant.' Don't get too comfortable. When you find success, remember that it's not comfort that got you to where you are.

Running the Play:

- Never stop learning and playing. The game changes every day.

- Remain humble.

- Be human, and relatable.

- Always give back. Answer the call.

- Be a strong representative and use your platform for good.

Tia Hopkins

Cybersecurity and Business Executive

Tia began her career as a high-speed internet installer in the early 2000s, which sparked her interest in the information technology field, and ultimately led to her focus on cybersecurity. She has spent more than two decades in the IT and IT Security industry and at the time of writing is a dual C-suite executive as Chief Cyber Resilience Officer & Field CTO. In addition to her day job, Tia is an adjunct professor of cybersecurity, a women's tackle football coach, a LinkedIn Learning Instructor, and serves on the board of two cybersecurity nonprofit organizations.

She holds several industry certifications including the CISSP, CISM, GSLC, and Boardroom Certified QTE (Qualified Technology Expert) in addition to a BS in

Information Technology, MS in Information Security and Assurance, MS in Cybersecurity and Information Assurance, and a Master of Business Administration. She is also pursuing a PhD in Cybersecurity Leadership.

Tia was recognized by SC Media as an outstanding educator in 2019, as well as one of The Software Report's Top 25 Women Leaders in Cybersecurity and Cyber Defense Magazine's Top 100 Women in Cybersecurity; both in 2020. In 2021, Tia was recognized as a Top Influencer in the Security Executives category by IFSEC Global, and #1 on Dark Reading's list of '8 More Women in Security You May Not Know but Should' in 2022. In 2023, she was named one of the Top 25 Leaders in Cybersecurity and received the U.S. President's Volunteer Service Award for the impact her work has had on the community.

Tia contributed a chapter to the book The Rise of Cyber Women: Volume 2 in 2021 and co-authored 'Hack the Cybersecurity Interview' with Ken Underhill and Chris Foulon in 2022. She is also the Founder of Empow(H)er Cybersecurity, a non-profit organization aimed at inspiring and empowering women of color to pursue cyberse careers.

LinkedIn: https://www.linkedin.com/in/yatiahopkins/

website: https://www.tiahopkins.com

CHAPTER 8

Black Women Are Late to the Party
"A story about getting out of your own
way to get into cyber"

By: Tennisha Martin

As the Black founder of an international cyber nonprofit organization, I get invited to many discussion panels. While some of my peers might shy away from being the token Black person, I'm here for it! If allowed to show up, I'm not only going to show up, but I'm going to show out. At these discussion panels, they tend to ask a lot of the same softball-type questions like "Who are you," "What do you do," and "Why do you do it?" And while the answer to those questions tells part of who I am and what I do, the question I believe genuinely represents me comes from a panel that asked about the defining moment in my career that contributed to the woman I am today. Let's get into it.

I'm the founder and Executive Director of BlackGirlsHack, a nonprofit created to help upskill and reskill people into cyber. You may have heard of us because I've made it my business to tell everyone who would listen in the three years since I founded the organization. I started BlackGirlsHack as an Instagram page to share resources and discounts on cyber training. Having gone to school at Carnegie Mellon University when Amazon was only a bookseller and buying textbooks might cost two to three hundred dollars per class, I learned to be on the lookout for a good discount. I was already looking for deals, so I'd share the ones I found on my journey, teaching myself to hack along the way. I'd share humble bundles (sets of ten to twenty PDF books, generally sold for around twenty dollars) and discounts on hands-on ethical hacking training. I started teaching hands-on workshops six days a week where I trained others using the little bit of knowledge I'd learned. I started making cyber friends and talking about BlackGirlsHack on Clubhouse and later on Twitter spaces, podcasts, and wherever someone would have me.

The defining moment of my career happened around October 2020, when one of my best friends, tired of me complaining about how much I hated my job and wanted to get into cyber, told me to get up and *do something* about it. Let me provide some background. I have always been a serial overachiever: I've got a Bachelor's degree in Electrical and Computer Engineering and five Masters degrees (IT, Health Care Policy and Management, Cyber, Digital Forensics, and an MBA). I had achieved all of the advanced level certifications in my chosen field of software testing/quality assurance and obtained certifications in project management and Service Management. My general approach to my job search was to be overqualified. As a Black woman in Tech, I was taught that I had to be better than everyone else to get the same opportunities, so I tend to be significantly "extra" when it comes to "staying ready, so I don't have to get ready." I didn't have a network, a mentor, or any concept of what a sponsor was. I was determined to do it all on my own without help from anyone, and despite 6 degrees and more than 15 certifications, I was failing at my job search and career change. I was making great money but I was no longer challenged or really interested in the work that I was doing. I had been in the same role for seven or eight years, and although I received annual two to three percent raises, I did not receive any promotions or advancement opportunities. I wasn't learning

any new skills in my job nor taking on new responsibilities–
I was just serving as a subject matter expert (SME), and
collecting checks. As a government contractor, the checks
were nice, but I wasn't happy with what I was doing and it
no longer brought me satisfaction. In reflecting on my life
up until that point, from the outside it might have looked
like I had it all: the amazing husband, the job, the
recognition– I was a rock star in a field that I didn't want to
be in anymore.

I was in the same position for about eight years and was
complacent and comfortable. In my job search to that point,
I'd changed the summary on my resume, added some
security-related buzzwords, and proceeded to become the
most significant obstacle of my desires. I wasn't able to get
a job in the cyber field because I was operating in a silo and
thought I could out-educate and out-certify the competition.
I was literally standing in my own way.

During this time, I had been a longtime member of the
Women's Society of Cyberjutsu and had been taking
occasional workshops and weekend classes with their
organization which had inspired me to dig deeper into cyber.
I had already completed a Master's degree in Cyber from
Johns Hopkins University and had just finished another

Master's in Digital Forensics from the University of Maryland, but I wasn't getting what I needed in terms of hands-on skills. My degrees were very much focused on theory, however didn't provide any hands-on keyboard skills. While I thought that my more than fifteen years of consulting experience in software testing, quality assurance, and security testing would make it easy for me to get a job in penetration testing, the job market proved otherwise. For the first couple of years of my applying to entry-level penetration testing jobs, I got a free education in the art of *ghosting*. I'd apply for jobs and hear nothing or in rare cases when I did hear something and was interviewed, there'd be radio silence after that. The only real feedback I got was that I was overqualified in some areas, yet for a job in penetration testing, I'd need more hands-on skills experience.

After sharing this feedback with my friend who again expressed to me that I wasn't living up to my potential and that if I wanted a different life, a different career, I needed to *do something* about it, I decided to get serious about developing my hands-on skills. I jumped head first into online training platforms like TryHackMe and Over the Wire, and Hack the Box. As I learned, I started hosting daily

Zoom sessions on Meetup where I invited other people who wanted to learn to come and learn with me. I didn't have all the answers, and sometimes I couldn't complete the challenges, but I was consistent and I made a material change about how my career would progress. I stopped talking about what I wanted and started taking action by prioritizing learning and developing the hands-on skills that I lacked. If you're a basketball fan, you'll understand that I started hitting the 'cyber' gym.

The defining moment of my career was not when I won an award and it wasn't when I got a big promotion (those things came later). The defining moment of my career was when I decided to get serious about my relationship with cyber and get out of my own way.

I started a nonprofit. I began recruiting other volunteers, and the workshops I was teaching were expanded to teach people hands-on keyboard skills, how to update their resume, and how, as a career changer, to represent the value that they bring to their future organizations. I began reaching out to people on LinkedIn to connect and tell them about my nonprofit and the work that we were doing. We partnered with training companies, like Rangeforce, our first organizational partner who provided their training for free, to give back. During the first few years, I met many people who were all trying to get into cyber. As I shared advice and genuinely listened to their journeys, it became clear that a common obstacle preventing many people from entering their new cyber careers was their tendency to push the door shut themselves. They, too, were all standing in their way.

Some people told themselves they couldn't afford to start over. For some, between work and life, they didn't have the time. Some weren't good at math in school and didn't think they could do it. And for some, they had been applying but not having any luck. The common theme that applied to most people that I talked to was that they were standing in their own way.

Change is hard for everyone. I'd argue that it's ten times harder the older you get. Stepping out of my comfort zone as an introvert was strangely, not the hardest part of my transformation. For me, the hardest part of my evolution was stepping past "I don't need anyone" smoothly into "I can't do it on my own, and I need help." For me, like many Black women, that innate, ingrained voice that told me to "trust no one" was loudest when I was telling people what I was trying to do to make a difference in this field. Imposter syndrome told me I wasn't qualified to lead anyone into anything, and I didn't deserve to be a leading voice in this space. I, like many people I encountered, was taking myself out of the game before I could even shoot a shot. As women, this looks like saying, "I don't meet enough of the qualifications to apply for this job", or "I don't have enough experience or the right experience", or "It's too hard to start over and do something new." With these types of excuses, we talk ourselves out of ever getting started. We're creating excuses for why we shouldn't even try.

Cyber as an industry started well over forty years ago, and if it was a party, we're way past the point of being fashionably late. Research shows that 24% of the cyber workforce are women and only 9% of the cyber workforce is Black. As a group, between 2-3% of the cyber workforce identify as Black women which means we're officially the endangered species of the industry. This may not seem like a problem to most, but I worked as a penetration tester/security consultant for almost nine months before I saw another woman hacker and about eighteen months before I saw another Black woman hacker (she joined after I referred her from BlackGirlsHack.)

Representation matters and realistically, the Black community is still telling our children to be doctors, lawyers, engineers, athletes, or actors. As a field, cyber doesn't have enough visible people doing big things, especially Black people–and if there's one thing that I know to be true, it's that you have to see it to be it. I heard a Black woman once say, "How can you ever desire to be an astronaut if you don't know space exists?" The same can be said about cyber. For most people in the Black community, especially if you're not already in the tech/cyberspace, if you've heard of a hacker, it was probably on TV.

Our community's lack of awareness about cyber, and careers within it, is a problem because cyber is a field that greatly benefits from the diversity of thought. As a penetration tester, thinking outside the box is not so much a motto, as it is a way of life. We need diversity in thought and approaches to problem-solving if we ever hope to be competitive on a global scale within this space. Our adversaries are diverse, their attacks are diverse, and if we want to be competitive, our cyber teams of the future need to represent that same diversity.

There's too much at stake, especially when we consider the bias that is embedded in systems such as facial recognition, healthcare systems, criminal justice systems, and hiring systems. Most of the biggest Artificial Intelligence systems for facial recognition have error rates as high as 31% for Black women. This technology is employed for law enforcement surveillance, airport passenger screening, and employment and housing decisions. What this means is that these systems are being taught bias, and have in some cases, life-or-death consequences for women of color. To combat these biases, we need people to do research in the areas of algorithms, machine learning, and artificial intelligence. To accomplish that we need the future scientists, mathematicians, and engineers of the world not only to be aware of the field but to understand the impact that our failure to address these issues will have on the future of our society.

Being late to the party means we are underrepresented in STEM-based undergraduate degrees, graduate degrees, and Ph.D. programs. It means we are underrepresented in the workforce, and in application pools, and we are underrepresented in the development of data for algorithms, machine learning, and artificial intelligence. It means when we talk ourselves out of the game before we've even played a minute, the downstream impacts are detrimental to the future of cyber. We need to get in the game and bring a few friends, too.

What I've found to be successful in spreading the word about the need for change was a strength in numbers. I'd tell someone all about BlackGirlsHack: about our hands-on training, our sponsors and grants, or available opportunities; and those people would tell other people, who in turn told others. Over time, BlackGirlsHack (BGH) grew; our membership expanded, and I got mentors, advisors, and sponsors who spoke my name in rooms I wasn't in. My network grew as my BGH squad grew, and people started getting certifications, jobs, and invaluable experiences. One of my mentors, Misty, convinced some of her friends in the mainframe penetration testing space to offer an exclusive one-week training program that provided exposure and hands-on skills to our squad. I met other nonprofit founders in this space like Mari Galloway, Tia Hopkins, and Talya Parker, who have become valued friends and part of my trusted circle. I reached out to other nonprofit organizations to partner with and bring workshops and trainings like, our first Security Plus study group, which brought hundreds of people out each week. Over time, I helped bring changes to my squad that upgraded their financial status, and the trajectory of their careers. I taught them to "shoot all shots" and to stop talking themselves out of applying for jobs and scholarships they didn't feel qualified or accomplished enough to deserve. I encouraged thousands of people to adopt a plan for world domination that not just invited them to live their best lives and achieve their biggest dreams, but to see themselves in greater positions and not settle for lives of complacency. I encouraged our members to dream bigger and to live a life out on the edge of uncertainty with the faith that what's for them, is for them.

The biggest accomplishment in my work with BlackGirlsHack is that we've developed a community of men, women, people of color, and people of the rainbow. Our community, our squad as I like to call them, are remarkable not because we're all trying to get into cyber or into tech fields, but because we represent a support system, a safe space where you can come as you are and grow and learn in a safe environment. Our value, as an organization, is that we meet our members where they are and provide direction, support, and training to help them to see what is possible. Because again, if you don't know that it exists, how can you want that for yourself?

While BlackGirlsHack provides training, resume reviews, and mock interviews to help people get started in careers in cyber, some of our most important work is our efforts to show the future hackers of the industry what is possible. We do this in a few ways, we have social media campaigns to show Black women in various careers within cyber and we hold weekly podcasts to help people understand what a day in the life of these careers looks like, but our biggest showcase of the possibilities is our yearly conference at Hacker Summer Camp in Las Vegas, Nevada. Girls Hack Village started in 2022 and was created to help showcase the research, careers, and experiences of women in the hacker/maker/breaker space. At Hacker Summer Camp, the yearly collection of the biggest cyber conferences in the world, there is a lack of representation in terms of the industry's "others". At DefCon, BlackHat, and BSides LV, other notable cyber conferences, women are noticeably missing, and minorities have historically been nearly nonexistent. From the keynotes, to the speakers and panels, to just walking the halls, seeing the industry's others has historically been few and far between. Girls Hack Village changed that. Our small space in the Flamingo Hotel was at standing-room capacity for each talk, panel, and workshop, and was an outstanding display of the research, experiences, and careers of women. It served, for both new and returning hackers, as a safe space to talk about life on the fringe of cyber. We brought 71 people of color to Hacker Summer Camp and provided to the thousands of people who came to our village exposure and endless ideas and opportunities. We delivered the message that we're here to stay. Girls Hack Village has expanded into a full-fledged inclusive conference and we're excited to bring SquadCon to the world at Hacker Summer Camp 2023.

The work that BlackGirlsHack and other organizations in the space are doing is not enough to get us to the party. With fifty percent of the organization between zero and five years into their cyber careers, our efforts are basically a Band-Aid on our broken heels to keep us upright. Tonight's party is almost over but the after-party and tomorrow's party will require us to come out in full force. To do this, we have to address the deficiencies at each stage of the employment pipeline. For kindergarteners through fifth graders that means establishing safe cyber hygiene and teaching them to protect themselves while online. For sixth through eighth graders, when students tend to form their STEM identities, it means being exposed to careers in cyber and being able to see people in the field who look like them and can serve as role models. For ninth through twelfth grade students that means helping the student to get prepared for careers in cyber and providing them with hands-on marketable skills and certifications. The reality is that when students graduate from high school not all of them want to go to college or can afford college. The recent decision by the Supreme Court of the United States to end Affirmative Action in college admissions, likely means there will be less diverse candidates in U.S. colleges. It means less diversity in the consulting firms, like the big four that frequently source from these schools, and for the cyber workforce, it means less educated people entering the cyber workforce.

Ensuring we have enough people for the party means meeting students and individuals where they are and giving them options outside of the college, military, and trade school paths. For the people who don't go to school, developing the pipeline for employment looks like helping them to get hands-on marketable skills and certifications to help them get started in careers in cyber. For those who go to college, they need help to get involved in Science, Technology, Engineering, Art, and Mathematical fields. At the master's level that looks like helping to fund research and interest in cyber industries at the intersection of areas that matter to them most. And at the PhD level help looks like sponsoring research that explores the algorithmic bias to develop machine learning and Artificial Intelligence systems that aren't built on decades of bias.

While BlackGirlsHack is developing programs and working with industry partners to feed into each of these stages of the pipeline, our greatest hurdle in a world with millions of cyber jobs remaining unfilled is to help those who are looking to get into the field to get out of their own way. It's helping them to expand their vision to see the possibilities, helping them build or establish a community, and helping to provide best practices and support. Our programs are meant to help the next generation of Black women take initiative, bet on themselves, and define themselves in the way that allows them to live their best lives and feed back into the communities to strengthen the pipeline. Most importantly, as they find themselves getting more certifications, more opportunities, and better jobs it's important that they reach back and give back and not be afraid to be vulnerable and talk to the next generations about the mistakes they made along the way.

If I'm talking to or about you, my call to action for you is to join our network and connect with us. That doesn't have to be BlackGirlsHack, but establish your own community, and get a squad. When people think of nine percent of Black people in the Cyber industry, they may see an industry that's not for them. What I see is the opportunity for change. What's keeping us from getting started is not a lack of capability; it's not a lack of intellect or creativity; it's a lack of perspective and understanding of the possibilities. So, if no one has invited you to the party, here's your official invitation to join. The only thing that is missing is you, your talent, and your intellect. And sister to sister (or brother), the only person that's holding you back is you. Stop making excuses, stop standing in your way, and get started today.

My hope for your life is that you will one day be able to identify and articulate the defining moment of your career. I hope that you will be able to rise above your circumstances and see where you've been and how you got here, and your future goals and the path to get there. To help you develop a plan of attack I've got 7 steps to help you get started.

1) **Develop a plan for world domination** – If you're reading this book in order to help you figure out your

direction, I encourage you to figure out where you're going. You can't stop and ask someone how to get there if you don't know where you're going. My world domination plan is to become the Chief Information Security Officer (CISO) of a Fortune 1000 company. That's what drives me each day. Once you figure out where you want to go, you need to develop a road map. That roadmap should contain what skills, experience, certifications, and knowledge you need to become a CISO, or whatever your goal is. Use LinkedIn to find people who are in that position today. What job did they have before that? What skills, experience, certifications, and knowledge did they need to get there? Continue that process until you get to a position close to where you're at today and that's your roadmap. Be intentional about the jobs you take, the assignments you take on and the certifications and education that you get so that it helps to get you further to that goal. There isn't just one right answer or path, but in order to get directions from your mentors, sponsors, or allies, you have to tell them you're going.

2) **Find your squad** – As an introvert, I can tell you that I tried for decades to elevate my life in a silo. I thought I

could out educate, out certify, and out qualify my competition into a well-paying job, but after almost 20 years in the technology industry, I've learned that's the exact **wrong** way to go about it. I have friends, but they're not in tech. We talk about our work in terms of widgets, but at a binary 1s and 0s level we don't know what each other does. There is value in being able to call other hackers and ask them about why my reverse shell isn't working and other ways that I can get into a network. There is value in having friends who you can bounce ideas off of and commiserate about the networks you couldn't break into. There's value in having a tribe. Even if that tribe is not "Black Girls Hack" (which is open to all regardless of gender or race), find a group of like-minded people who can identify with what you're trying to do and can support you as you do it.

3) **Define your brand** – When I was growing up, the internet didn't exist and your reputation was what defined you when you walked into a room. In the age of the internet, most people you will interact with don't know who you are. You have the unique ability on LinkedIn, on Instagram, on Twitter, or wherever you find yourself in the *cyber streets* to identify who you are

and what you're about. Use your social media presence to say who you are, even before you get there. I'm not talking about putting "Aspiring Penetration Tester" in your LinkedIn about section, I'm talking about putting "Penetration Tester for mobile, network, and mainframe systems" as you work to level up in those areas. I'm talking about developing a portfolio of work that establishes your skills. Develop a sixty-second elevator pitch to tell people who you are and what you're trying to do. When you do this, you'll find that people will surprise you and when they see opportunities in your wheelhouse, they'll let you know about it. There's strength in numbers and community.

4) **Identify a network of Mentors, Sponsors, Allies** - Much of the success and growth that "Black Girls Hack" has experienced is largely due to the people behind the scenes who help to provide me with direction, advice, and best practices based on their experience. Mari Galloway, one of the authors of this book and Executive Director (ED) of Women's Society of Cyberjutsu has been one of my most influential mentors and friends. Despite the fact that Mari is younger than I am, she has way more certifications and knowledge in this space and

she has never hesitated to share with me. She's shared her experience running a nonprofit with me, telling me about the roadblocks she's faced along the way and how to avoid them. Tia Hopkins, the founder of EmpowHer Cybersecurity has been the same. As a C-level executive, she has a wealth of experience and is already in the upper echelon of the industry. She understands what is needed and is generous with her wisdom. I mentioned my mentor Misty Decker earlier and I have mentors, like Mary Chaney, Esq of Minorities in Cybersecurity among countless others.. You will find that your mentors, sponsors, and allies will be an important part of your journey and they are necessary to help you avoid mistakes. We don't need to repeat history if we can make it.

5) **Prioritize your plan** – It's one thing to say you want to be a penetration tester, a hacker, or a CISO one day, and it's another thing to actually do it. It's easy to have five, ten, or even fifteen years go by talking about a goal that you never achieved. You eat each day, and hopefully, you're hydrated and you make time for your family, your friends, and exercise, and things that make you happy. Prioritize your future. It's important to live in the

moment, but also to plan for the future. Carve out an hour each day to study, to hack, to read up on policies, to do something that will get you closer to the goal. Your family needs you and is counting on you, but "future you" is counting on you as well.

6) **Give and Reach Back** – A lot of people feel like they're not at the point in their lives where they can give back. I've had people tell me "When I get my job in cyber, when I start making real money, when I become a CISO, then I'm going to give back or help people the way they helped me." You don't have to wait until you've achieved success to give back. I started teaching workshops on how to hack before I really knew what hacking was. Whatever I learned I taught to someone else because it helped them, and teaching it helped me to understand what I was learning. It's never too soon to start giving back and it doesn't have to be financial. You can volunteer to give a workshop or a training, or to mentor someone just starting up. Don't be a leech–make sure that for as much as you're taking, you are also giving back.

7) **Define Your Legacy** – How do you want to be remembered? What do you want people to say about how you lived your life when you are gone? I am intentional about what I do and how I give back because I want to be remembered as someone who helped someone else's life to be better. Be remembered as someone who showed up to the party and made it better.

When I'm asked to be the token Black woman at a conference, on a panel, or in a room, I jump at the opportunity. Because the reality is, to get a seat at the table you've got to at least be in the room. Since getting out of my own way, I've had the opportunity to be mentored and sponsored by some amazing people. I've had the opportunity to build friendships and bonds with people who are committed to making a change in my love language of giving back, and I've had my name spoken in rooms that I didn't know existed. I'm working each day to expand my network, expand my squad, and stay out of my own way, but I've got to be honest with you about something; I can't do it all on my own. I need your help. We're late to the party, so get up and get dressed, but put on your comfortable shoes, I'm out of Band-Aids.

Tennisha Martin

Founder and Executive Director | BlackGirlsHack

Tennisha Martin is the founder and Executive Director of BlackGirlsHack (BGH Foundation), a national cyber nonprofit organization dedicated to providing education and resources to underserved communities and increasing the diversity in cyber. BlackGirlsHack provides its members with resources, mentorship, direction, and training required to enter and excel in the cyber field. Tennisha has a Bachelor's degree in Electrical and Computer Engineering from Carnegie Mellon University and Master's degrees in IT, Healthcare Policy and Management, Cyber Security, Digital Forensics, and Business Administration. She has worked in a consulting capacity for over 15 years in penetration testing, project management, risk management, audit, information assurance, quality assurance, software development, and testing roles. Tennisha is a professor of computer science and cyber at an HBCU, co-author of "Breaking Barriers & Building Bridges," mentor, speaker, and an advocate for diversity in cyber and the executive suites.

LinkedIn: https://www.linkedin.com/in/tennisha/

Twitter: https://twitter.com/misstennisha

Website: https://www.tennisha.com

CHAPTER 9

Daring to Shine - Don't Let Humility Be Your Hurdle to Success

By: Shinesa Cambric

For as long as I can remember, I've enjoyed a challenge - taking opportunities that others were afraid of, felt were impossible or complex, or that would make them stand out. In the sixth grade, I recall seeing a note from my teacher to my parents reading, "Shinesa loves being challenged," and I've found it to be consistently true about me. In college, I chose Computer Science as my major and dove into technology, mainly because it presented the most opportunity and was what I saw as the more challenging path. Being a Black female in computer science, I was often surrounded by mostly white men in the room, whether they be my peers or my professors. In many cases, I was the only female or the only person of color, and in all my years of study for my degree, I came across only one other Black female computer science student. Despite being different, and maybe partially because of it, it was important to prove to myself and those around me that I could do this. Being a person who loves challenges means that I've spent a lot of time going after things because they hadn't been done before or people assumed they couldn't be done, especially by someone who looked like me. To this day, I love a good underdog story and now thrive on being underestimated.

When I graduated college, I took a job in application development. As part of the role, I raised my hand to learn more about application security and work as a liaison with the security team. Taking on this opportunity led to a job with that team and a career spanning multiple cyber domains, including identity and access management, security architecture, and compliance. This was well before these fields became the hot career choices they are now. At the time, these were roles and careers no one wanted or saw value in, but these were all necessary functions for a successful company. The Sarbanes-Oxley Act had just passed, and I knew the law would lead to significant opportunities for learning and growth, and it did. It led me to stints at large and small companies, ranging from consumer goods to aerospace and defense, and with each opportunity, I remained a results-driven high performer.

Everywhere I've worked, I've always been the one people called on to execute and get things done. I kept my head down, quietly did what was asked (and more), and was a top problem solver across the company. So it came as a shock to me one day when a manager told me I did excellent work, but I would never be promoted to leadership levels beyond my current position because no one knew who I was. It shocked me because I was the go-to person who knew and spent time regularly with leaders across our business unit. When others needed a security solution, they came to me. I was an idea generator and an architect of what we had in place. I helped many others in building skills and delivering with excellence. I was getting impactful work done, and I had assumed that work was being valued and acknowledged without me amplifying it. I was checking all the boxes and had strong relationships with my peers and coworkers across the organization, so I didn't understand the rationale behind my manager's statement, which hurt. After hearing this, I had to choose what to do with that comment. I could have easily gotten defensive, angry, or frustrated. Instead, I decided to reflect and focus on self-awareness of what could be holding me back, dissect and digest the "message behind the message", and ask myself what new challenge I needed to take on. I had to uncover how it could be possible for me to work so hard, know everyone in my division and many across the organization, but still not be "known." I realized my manager's comment was the wake-up call I needed to focus on investing in myself and my personal brand. I needed to be more visible and incredibly more intentional with my career choices, successes, and aspirations. I realized I hadn't even scratched the surface of my potential, and my new challenge was making sure no one could limit that. I had been doing great work, but I wasn't doing a great job of taking credit for the work that I was doing. I wasn't making sure decision-makers knew my accomplishments and spoke about them in the rooms I wasn't in. I hadn't promoted the excellent work I had already done or my capabilities and vision for achieving even greater things.

I came into the working world with the impression that good work speaks for itself. It can up to a point, but my manager's comment made clear to me that you need to give your good work and your career intentions a platform. As a young girl, I was taught to "be seen and not heard" and grew up as quiet, shy, and introverted, so being vocal and boastful about my achievements did not come easy or naturally to me. Now, I realize that to make it into the spaces I want to be in and have the far-reaching positive influence I want to have, I have to speak up. Other leaders didn't view me as promotion-ready because I failed to speak up and use my voice. I needed to be bold in communicating the impact that I was making, and I wasn't my own cheerleader when it came to bringing awareness of my value to the organization. Instead, I was quiet and humble, thinking that others would do this for me or "see it" from the work that I had done. I didn't realize that my "humility" (which was really fear of speaking up in disguise) was now becoming the hurdle keeping me from my goals. I was afraid of what others would say or think if I chose to take ownership and "brag" about my accomplishments. Over time, I had allowed my mindset of taking on challenges to be minimized by passively allowing others to dictate how my career would go. After assessing who I had been and who I wanted to become, I saw getting over my "humility" and letting my light shine as the new challenge defining my life and now my legacy.

After that career experience, my eyes were officially opened. No longer could I or would I be passive. No longer could I or would I be quiet. No longer could I or would I let fear and humility cause me to shrink back from my potential. And it wasn't just about me–it was also about others like me who may have received a similar message of being "unknown". I decided that this little light of mine, I'm going to let it shine. For me, this meant getting clear and intentional about my career and personal goals. A primary driving goal for me was to open the door to new spaces for people from diverse backgrounds and encourage them that they belonged. A second but equally important goal was to be a visible representation of a Black woman leading the way through those doors, succeeding, and showing what's possible. Both require being visible, reaching out to the community, being vocal across a broad network, and building a personal brand reflecting success both within and outside of the company I work for.

I've learned that building a personal brand within your company primes you to be considered for strategic opportunities. It helps ensure leaders within your organization are aware of the value and impact you've already delivered, your career goals, how those goals align with your organization's future plans, and your potential to succeed and deliver on those goals as you advance to new levels. When you build a personal brand within your organization, you dare show up, stand tall, shine the light on your skills, and refuse to be a quiet kept secret. Your brand builds increased influence and opportunities and opens up options to elevate your career. The impact of being silent about your work and choosing not to shine your light has ripple effects. I understand the desire to play it safe, it's exactly what I had done for more years than I should have. In cyber, often, when you come into these spaces and you're the minority, the tendency is to tiptoe around as if you're just happy to be here, refusing to ruffle any feathers or rock the boat. It's critical to challenge that thinking and remind ourselves (and the organization) that we are an asset and start showing up that way. Building your personal brand and making intentional choices to be visible and heard means showing up in the room with the courage and mindset that you deserve to be there. Show up and speak up as if what you have to say matters because it does - not just for you, but the many others who may be watching your journey and looking to you as a role model. As a Black woman, getting others in these spaces is essential. When we are included in the conversation, we get to influence the decisions being made and help reduce bias; we can weigh in on the rules and policies being put into place that need to reflect our voices and perspectives. And as we gain access to those spaces, we need to open the door for the next woman behind us.

If you work as an employee, building your brand inside your organization is important, and doing so externally is just as important. For me, building my external brand has helped me to share the challenges I've overcome, make a community and global impact, and give back to others through mentoring, training, and encouragement. Being visible and sharing my story has allowed me to speak into the lives of others and encourage them, which has led to one of the best rewards: multiple people beginning and thriving in a new career within cyber and not being afraid to use their voice and platform to share their success.

The statistics for women within cyber are low, and for Black women, building an intentional career within cyber has been almost unheard of. By daring to be different, speaking up, and taking on this challenge, I've empowered myself to be a representation for others to expand their vision of possibilities for successful, high-impact careers for young Black women and women of color.

As I build my personal brand, it's vital for me to be clear about what I want to accomplish, know the opportunities and possibilities I want available to me, and then go out and do the work to make it happen. One of the key career benefits of building your brand through standing up, speaking up, and being visible, is that it unlocks new levels of growth and expansion in the areas you've intentionally expressed interest in. Shining brightly helps you to grow your network, attract all sorts of opportunities, and position yourself so that others can find and connect you with those opportunities.

In addition to doing the work to take advantage of these new opportunities, building up my mindset (and, for me, faith) has played an essential role in my success. Overcoming challenges and stretching yourself to reach new goals won't come and definitely won't be sustained without the right mindset. You will run into roadblocks, negative perceptions, and hurdles to overcome, and you'll have to make a choice. You have the power to choose what you want to believe and whether you will allow that belief to either empower you to move forward or hold you back.

Building my personal brand has led to dream job opportunities that allow me to make a global impact, share my insights and guidance with others through mentorship, and expand my network reach. I've had the opportunity to speak to a packed house at the RSA conference, one of the largest cyber conferences in the world. I've spoken at SANS, have been a regular YouTube host for the OWASP DevSlop special project, and continue to be a requested speaker and contributor to blogs and podcasts, allowing me to influence others through sharing my personal and professional perspectives across various global platforms. I directly influence the cyber industry by contributing as a subject matter expert for certification exams and training content, serving as a board member of cyber non-profit organizations, and developing content and course creation delivered through well-known educational organizations. As a result of building my brand, I accepted the opportunity to complete a goal and write a best-selling first-of-its-kind cyber technical book. The book was a featured best seller for Amazon and continues to be a leading seller for the publishing company; this has also led to opportunities to author and co-author additional content. My influence has led to being recruited as an advisor to a startup that has been achieving great success by leveraging the ideas I've brought forward and opening up various new opportunities for others in my network. As a quiet person by nature, none of these things have been easy, but building up the courage and intentionality to do them has been worth it. This influence and impact would not have come had I not stepped past fear, chosen to be visible, chosen to publicly share my ideas, and said, "YES" to the challenge of shining my light. Once you accept that you have an impact to make and a legacy to leave, you must also take action. "Everything you've ever wanted is sitting on the other side of fear" – George Addair

In our current digital environment, being shy or not speaking up could be detrimental to your career. When daring to shine, you must commit to taking a bold stance in sharing your talent and gifts to make the impact you want to see in the world. Sharing your story, amplifying your voice, letting people know who you are, and sharing your goals will be an asset to you within your career field. Whether you decide to elevate within your current career and work your way up the ladder, or take a step further and leverage your brand for industry recognition and other opportunities, you have to be courageous enough to dare to be different and stand out.

Shining your light and highlighting your victories and impact is not about being arrogant, entitled, lacking gratitude, or even lacking (genuine) humility. It's about owning your accomplishments, boldly acknowledging them, and sharing with the world the distinct value you bring to the table. It's about sharing your "shine" with the world. As a person of faith, I believe that we are called to be lights in the world – and light isn't meant to be hidden or dimmed; it's meant to be visible and a beacon for all to see. I believe we are all here FOR a purpose and ON purpose, and you can't fully execute that if you shrink back into the shadows with your head down, lacking intentionality and allowing others to be in the driver's seat of your career.

You have unique gifts that you bring to the world - don't be afraid to share them. No one benefits when we shrink back. The path for others becomes hidden if no "light" is shining for them to see it. And if you don't want to do it for yourself, think about how your willingness to show up and shine can inspire the lives of others looking for hope. Keep yourself from playing small when you are capable of so much more!

So what does it look like for YOU to dare to be different – to step past fear and take your place on the stage? You'll have to be willing to be a first, be an only, and take on new challenges with courage. You must show up for yourself and step out of your comfort zone to flourish and shine. When it comes to why you aren't already sharing your successes or choosing to be visible, you'll need to have an honest conversation with yourself. Decide if you're really being humble or, like me, you have just been scared to shine, celebrate your wins with others, or let your potential and ambitions be known. Ask yourself, in the rooms you want to be in, who knows the impact you're making and is willing to advocate for you when there is an opportunity that aligns with your career and personal goals, and do they even know your goals? Commit to being fully engaged and intentional about bringing your light and gifts to the world.

Refuse to dim your light because of what you assume others may think, as I did early in my career. You may not realize who needs to see or hear from you to be the source of encouragement and inspiration that helps them overcome challenges. I love the field of cyber as a way of protecting others, using my passions and gifts - and being paid well to do so. I work daily to step into the challenge of being seen and encouraging girls worldwide that there is a place for them in cyber.

Don't be shy about who you are, what makes you different, and what skills you bring to the table. Often you hear the phrase "See it and be it". What I've learned is that sometimes you must take a different approach. There will be times, like for me, when there might not be an example for you to follow, and you need to be the first. Don't limit yourself to only what you see. If I had done that, there would have been so many opportunities for impact and influence I would have missed out on. I encourage you to "dream it and go be it". Embracing challenges has helped me to also embrace that I'm often the "first" or the "only" in the space I'm in, and that's okay. I'm happy to be there to open the door for others to come through. Role models are important, and sometimes you need to be a role model to yourself.

A crucial step in building your personal brand is the decision to rise and shine for YOURSELF. Know your "why" and choose how you will dare to be different. I mentioned a few of my goals for building my brand and creating visibility for my accomplishments. My ultimate "why" is to use my skills and giftings for the power of good. To do that means I needed to amplify those gifts and no longer be a "best-kept secret". This allows me to encourage and inspire others, be a role model, and leave my mark on the world by influencing and having my voice heard. When you see fingerprints on a piece of glass, you know someone has been there. In the same way, I want to leave my fingerprint on the world. I want to leave evidence of my unique sparkle. Where are you choosing to leave fingerprints behind? How are you making it evident to your company and the world that you have been here and have left your mark?

To get started on your journey to show up and shine by building your personal brand and influence, there are a few actions that I recommend you take:

- Commit to updating your LinkedIn profile (and keeping it up to date) and building your professional network. Ensure your profile showcases what you've done and where you want to take your career. Make sure your profile aligns with what you want to be known for so that others can connect you with opportunities that align with that.

- Challenge yourself to be visible regularly using your social platform of choice. You can start small - repost your thoughts on other content and current events that align with your goal and mission of what you want to be known for. When posting, be authentic, genuine, and consistent. Trying to build an image around something that is not authentic to you will instantly become work and a second job. Staying true to what resonates with you will allow you to also resonate with others. Authentically shine your light within your industry; don't worry about the number of "likes" or "comments". If you share in a way that's true to you, in time those will come. Don't feel the need to copy someone else's style. Take similar steps within your organization to be a "thought leader" by sharing knowledge and learning with your peers and senior leaders.

- Celebrate yourself and allow others to celebrate with you by sharing your accomplishments. Accept the compliments and encouragement, and don't minimize them. In the same way, be sure to celebrate the success of others within your network. At work, share with your leaders about the certifications you've passed, new courses you've completed, or the non-profit organizations you're volunteering with.

- Connect with one new person regularly. You must build your network both inside and outside your place of work and be sure to ask them for industry or career insights and share your own. This should be a two-way relationship.

- Consistently work on building your brand. Pick two to three adjectives of what you want to be known for and build your brand around that (both within your company and externally). As you work to become more visible, incorporate aspects that align with those adjectives as much as possible, even using them when you speak to describe yourself and your work. Ask others how they see your image aligning/misaligning with those adjectives, and don't limit yourself to one person's opinion. Be sure your feedback comes from those who have a track record of offering good insights and establishing a reputable brand for themselves.

- Continue to raise your hand for opportunities and step into challenges. Raising your hand will often get you into rooms and help you build skills you might not otherwise get. Don't let fear stop you because you may be the "first" or "only". Do it, open the door to others, and follow up by shining a light on your impact.

In addition to the guidance above, there are a few questions you should spend time reflecting on. When my manager told me I'd never be promoted, these are things I had to answer for myself that kick-started my journey to letting my light shine.

- Why am I doing what I'm doing?

- Where does my current path lead?

- What do I need to be more intentional about this month, quarter, year?

- What does success look like to me?

- What is my end goal? What matters to me?

- What's my value proposition? What skills do I bring to the table?

- What legacy do I want to leave?

- How are the signals I'm sending to others (personal brand/reputation) aligned with the goals I want to achieve?

Once you've answered these questions for yourself, decide that from here on out, you will be confident, bold, visible, and on brand. Now that you know my story and the difference courageously building a personal brand has made for me, you are no longer allowed to shrink. Decide to shine instead!

Shinesa Cambric

Cybersecurity Innovator | Microsoft

Shinesa Cambric (CCSP, CISSP, CISM, CDPSE) is an award-winning cyber innovator, emerging technology leader, author of the best-selling book "Cloud Auditing Best Practices": https://a.co/d/bFMtWk3, lead developer for the newly released ISACA GCP audit program and creator of an enterprise auditing course available through the O'Reilly learning platform.

As a senior leader in product management at Microsoft, Shinesa currently directs a team focused on designing innovative solutions using AI and machine learning to help global organizations identify, detect, and respond to developing threats, with two patents pending. Her experience includes the strategic technical design and implementation of identity protection solutions, building insider threat programs, and providing unique subject matter expertise on the intersection of governance, risk, and compliance with IT and application security. She is passionate about leading and supporting global teams, defining roadmaps for successful identity and access management programs, and architecting security strategies for emerging technologies. Shinesa is also an advocate for diversity in cyber and uses her unique perspective to advise non-profit boards and startups. She contributes to the growth and understanding of cyber by sharing her expertise with certifying organizations such as CompTIA, where she is an exam content subject matter expert for CompTIA Project+ and CySA+ (Cybersecurity Analyst) certifications; contributor and subject matter expert for the CyberSAFE certification with CertNexus; and contributor and reviewer of the Zero Trust training and certification content with Cloud Security Alliance.

Shinesa's professional guidance is featured in the book "97 Things Every Information Security Professional Should Know" and eBook "Shifting Security Left". Her work can be found in global IT industry forums such as SANS, RSAC Podcast and Conference, ITSP Magazine and podcast, BrightTALK, Secure Software Summit, DevOps.com, KBKast, Women In Identity, Top Cyber News Magazine, and Women In Security Magazine.

Shinesa has a Computer Science degree from Louisiana State University. She is the training lead for the Dallas chapter of the Women's Society of Cyberjutsu, the 2023 Rising Star award recipient and member of Cloud Girls, and serves on the board and conference organizing committee for fwd:cloudsec.

LinkedIn: https://www.linkedin.com/in/shinesa-cambric/

Twitter: https://twitter.com/Gleauxbalsecur1

CHAPTER 10

Securing Possibilities

By: Zinet Kemal

"You are built not to shrink down to less but to blossom into more. To be more splendid. To be more extraordinary." ~ Oprah Winfrey

---

It was the middle of winter in January of 2013 when our long flight landed in snowy Minnesota at about 7 p.m. The bitter cold greeted us as we stepped off the plane, and the unfamiliar surroundings seemed to magnify our sense of uncertainty. I was seven months pregnant, traveling with my almost three-year-old son and my husband, as we embarked on a new chapter of our lives. Choosing Minnesota as our new home was a leap of faith. We had barely known anyone in the States, except for my husband's high school classmate who graciously welcomed us, but had to leave just four days after our arrival to visit her family in Ethiopia. And so, after those initial four days on a new continent, we found ourselves standing on the threshold of creating a new life while simultaneously navigating the uncharted waters of a foreign land.

Born and raised in Addis Ababa, Ethiopia, I followed a path that led me to law school. After completing my education, I worked as a legal intern at a non-governmental organization, dedicating my efforts to children's rights in Africa. However, at the age of 21 marriage and motherhood called me to take a step back from my career for a year to nurture my firstborn and family. Following my hiatus from the workforce caring for my son for over a year, I then worked at a government investment agency as a legal expert for two years advising foreign investors. Through that role, I traveled to different countries including Zambia, Qatar, and South Africa to make legal bilateral negotiations on behalf of the government agency. I also had the pleasure of working with disciplined and talented colleagues and leaders. It was during this time that my husband and I made the life-changing decision to move to the United States in search of better opportunities. Winning a diversity visa allowed us the chance to travel and work abroad, setting the stage for a new beginning and opportunity. Although I had a scholarship opportunity to pursue a graduate degree in Tanzania, I had to discontinue my studies after only earning a postgraduate certificate in International Trade Policy and Law from ESAMI -Trade Policy Training in Africa with great distinction.

A few months into our arrival in the US, while my husband sought out employment to support our family, I settled into my role as a mother to our toddler and prepared for the arrival of our second child. But within me, there was a yearning to go back to school, rebuild my career, to contribute to the world in a different way, and to explore new possibilities that aligned with my passion. With my fascination for its power to simplify lives and solve everyday problems, I made the daunting decision to pursue an education in technology. In the fall of that year, I enrolled in a local community college to embark on an associate degree program in computer programming. I had absolutely no math or any computing background when I made that decision. I know, what was I thinking?

Overcoming my lack of mathematical or any computing background, I persevered and graduated two years later with an associate degree in computer programming. Despite this accomplishment, I felt a lingering uncertainty about marketing my newfound skill and confidence in a new field, in a new country, and new continent. Determined to bridge the gap, I transferred to a four-year degree program to earn my bachelor's degree in computer science.

My self-doubt and perceptions proved to be unfounded as I excelled in all my math courses including advanced ones, shattering the preconceived limitations that had plagued me since high school – that I shouldn't be in any fields that involve math or natural science.

The road was not without obstacles, and there were moments when the circumstances seemed far from convenient. However, I firmly believe that relentless determination offers access to opportunities and enables us to remain relevant and valuable in our chosen industries.

Please allow me to humbly introduce myself. I am an immigrant from Ethiopia and a mother to four amazing children. With audacious spirit, I fearlessly ventured from the legal field to embrace the Cyber industry. I currently work as a Cloud Security Engineer for a Fortune 500 organization. I am a multi-award-winning cyber professional, children's book author, and TEDx speaker. As a first generation with a master's degree in Cybersecurity from Georgia Tech University and a foundation rooted in both Computer Science and Law, I radiate passion for technology and cyber security. Not only am I an award-winning children's book author, but also a beacon of inspiration to young minds yearning to explore about online safety and cyber careers. Through my published works, I strive to empower and ignite the imaginations of these young curious minds. Along this arduous path, I have been blessed with the recognition of multiple esteemed awards. Each award an emblem of pride in my chosen field including the 2023 honoree for Minneapolis/St. Paul Business Journal '40 under 40', Georgia Tech University Ivan Allen Legacy Awards from graduate school, SANS Difference Makers Award Best Book of the Year, Women Who Code Applaud Her Awards in Security, 2022 SC Media Women in IT Security Cyber Advocate, 2022 CyberScoop Most Inspiring Up and Comer, and 2021 Team Women's WaveMakers Award – Uncharted Territory Honoree.

The echoes of my story and messages of my books have resounded through the airwaves, reaching the ears of those who seek both inspiration and enlightenment. Media outlets such as Good Morning America, BBC, ABC News, Yahoo! News, 11Alive, and CBS Minnesota have featured me and my children's books.

A little spark of Cyber

In my undergraduate years studying computer science, one concept remained shrouded in mystery to me, cybersecurity. I had never heard of it as a discipline or field of study, not even as a required course for a single class. It wasn't until late 2017, when I stumbled upon an elective course titled 'Introduction to Information Security,' that the doors of this world swung wide open. Little did I know that this encounter would mark the genesis of a journey that would shape not only my career but also my perception of the boundless possibilities that exist within the cybersecurity space.

The professor of this class, Professor Faisal Kaleem, possessed an unwavering passion for the subject matter. With an infectious enthusiasm, he shared his knowledge and experiences, igniting sparks of curiosity within our minds. It was during one of these engaging sessions that he revealed an extraordinary opportunity: coaching candidates to represent the University for the Minnesota Collegiate Cyber

Defense Competition (CCDC). Eager to explore, I enthusiastically signed up, joined by a cohort of like-minded students.

Beneath the weight of responsibilities as a full-time student, a part-time IT intern, and a mother of three young children, I embarked on a grueling journey of self-preparation. Each Saturday and while the world slept, I delved deep into the intricate web of cyber, honing my skills and expanding my knowledge. The path was challenging, but my determination propelled me forward toward the opportunity that awaited. Months flew by like fleeting shadows, and the day of reckoning arrived. Amongst a team of eight remarkable students, I stood as a representative of my university in the CCDC competition. This immersive experience thrust me into the heart of the near real-world security industry, where blue, red, and white teamers interacted. Within the simulated environment of a business besieged by adversaries, I discovered the art of defending against relentless attacks. When the dust settled and the winners were announced, the resounding applause echoed. The university I represented secured a remarkable third place among esteemed Minnesota colleges and universities in 2018. This experience and achievement became the catalyst that propelled me forward, fueling my insatiable hunger for knowledge through certifications, gaining new skills, pushing through IT internships, my first cyber role then to subsequent ones – all to gain experience towards a future to secure possibilities.

Why cyber became my passion

As I delved deeper into the vast expanse of the cybersecurity space, my fascination for technology intertwined seamlessly with the ever-evolving nature of the industry. The constant flux of digital solutions and emerging threats became challenges that beckoned me to push the boundaries of my abilities. The exhilaration that coursed through my veins when I witnessed the impact of my knowledge and skills in protecting people and organizations from the threats of cyberspace was immeasurable. The idea that my contributions will make the online world a safer place fueled my sense of purpose and ignited within me a motivation to strive for excellence. Yet, as my journey progressed, a disheartening truth revealed itself, a gender gap yawned wide, and diversity remained elusive within the industry. This revelation became a call, resonating deep within my being. It stirred a desire to transcend the boundaries imposed by societal norms, to shatter glass ceilings, and dismantle the barriers that prevented underrepresented individuals from tapping into their full potential. I yearned to be an inspiration and role model for others who looked like me, empowering them to dare to dream and embrace the boundless opportunities that awaited them in the cybersecurity space.

With unyielding determination, I became an advocate for diversity and inclusion, making contributions to bridge the gaps and reshape the narrative of the industry. As my career continued to ascend, I remained resolute in my mission to inspire, educate, and empower the next generation. I embraced opportunities to share my knowledge, experiences, and insights, nurturing a generation of cyber professionals who would transform the landscape and reduce the gender and diversity gap. Through my endeavors as an author, speaker, and advocate, I continue to kindle the flames of passion in aspiring professionals from underrepresented backgrounds, empowering them to break free from convention and pursue their dreams. As I gaze upon the horizon, the possibilities that lie within the field of cyber are infinite.

Embarking on a cyber career journey as a Black immigrant Muslim hijabi woman has instilled in me a deep passion for helping others secure possibilities in this field. Through my experiences, I have identified six principles that can empower individuals to thrive in cyber - the power of education, strategic time management, seizing opportunities, building a personal brand, problem-solving mindset, and leaning on mentors and allies.

Six principles to Secure cyber possibilities

1. The Power of Education

Education has been the cornerstone of my journey, enabling me to transcend the limitations imposed by poverty and societal expectations. Growing up in Ethiopia, my parents instilled in me the belief that education was the key to a brighter future, and they spared no effort to ensure my siblings and I had access to relatively quality education, often making sacrifices to ensure our access. Initially, I set my sights on a legal career, motivated by the respect and promise it held. Throughout law school, I honed my skills as a debater, representing my university in prestigious moot court competitions on a global stage. However, when life led me to the U.S., I found myself at a crossroads, questioning my chosen path. In a turn of events, my passion for technology sparked a new direction that would reshape my career and purpose.

I embarked on a journey of continuous education, from an associate degree in computer programming to a bachelor's degree in computer science then a master's degree in cybersecurity as a first generation to earn the highest level of degree at Georgia Tech University. Balancing motherhood and academia was no small feat, but it fueled my determination to excel and reach my goal.

Today, as I reflect upon my journey, I am humbled and proud of the accomplishments I have achieved as a multi-award-winning cyber professional, children's book author, TEDx speaker, and advocate. I stand as a living testament to the endless possibilities that education can unlock. It is my unwavering mission to inspire and empower others, particularly women, and to serve as a role model for my own children.

From the young girl who traversed long distances to school on crowded public transportation, being responsible for her three younger siblings while fighting severe motion sickness, multiple harassers on the way to and from school, and poverty; to the accomplished professional I am today, I have witnessed firsthand the profound impact of knowledge.

Education is not just about acquiring facts and figures; it is a transformative journey that expands our horizons and opens doors we never knew existed. It is through knowledge that we can transcend boundaries, challenge expectations, and shape our own destinies.

Formal education may not be the sole path, and not for everyone, but for me along with other means, such as targeted industry certifications, and internship opportunities, it opened doors to broader career opportunities and ensured readiness for the future and what lies ahead. Be strategic in your journey to education; it doesn't have to be expensive. In the past nine years since I immigrated to the U.S., I have earned three degrees, debt-free. I made sure I evaluated the worth, looked for and utilized scholarships, and started from local community college then transferred credits. If you wish to continue further, make sure your employer supports paying for it too.

As I continue to advocate for the power of education, I hope to inspire others to embrace their own journeys, no matter their background or circumstances.

2. Strategic Time Management - Maximizing Productivity

I often get asked, "How do you find the time to do all the things you do?"

There is no secret. Just like everyone else, I have 24 hours in a day. But one thing I live by is never postpone anything I can do today for tomorrow. Trust me, tomorrow comes with its own challenges and opportunities.

As an immigrant mother of four young children, I recognized the importance of spending my time strategically. I set clear and achievable goals for both short and long term and create a plan of action to reach them. I also prioritize tasks and focus on the most important ones to make the most of my time and achieve desired outcomes.

Self-discipline is a key aspect of utilizing time effectively. It means dodging distractions and staying focused on goals. That's how I was able to pursue full-time classes, a part-time internship, a number of relevant security certifications, or publish three children's books while parenting four young children, or working full time. Now, I don't really believe in work-life balance, rather it's about learning to continually prioritize and re-prioritize.

It is also important to know when to take a break and recharge. Taking breaks is a crucial part of being productive, as it allows us to recharge our energy and come back to our goals with renewed focus and motivation. That is something I always wanted to get better at to avoid burnout. If you push too hard and don't know your limits your body will crash, and your mental health will suffer. No job is worth your mental health. Reflecting on your progress and evaluating your journey regularly is important in best utilizing your time. This includes reviewing your goals and determining if you are on track to achieve them, as well as identifying areas for improvement and taking the necessary steps to make changes.

3. Seizing Opportunities - Advocating for Self

As a career changer and as someone who came from not having a lot of opportunities, I understand the importance of seizing opportunities and the value of advocating for self. The field of cybersecurity is constantly evolving, and it is crucial for you to be proactive and open to new possibilities to advance and succeed.

One way for you to seize opportunities is to be proactive and be on the lookout for career opportunities that align with your career goals. This can be achieved by looking out for roles within your organization that are close to where you are looking to transition or connecting with professionals on LinkedIn with roles that you are aspiring to hold. When I was an IT intern at a local government back in 2017, I looked out, networked, and ventured out on opportunities to intern in three departments as an IT intern. This allowed me to get closer to my goals, which led me to my first full-time role.

It's not just about recognizing opportunities, it's also about being able to effectively communicate your goals, and aspirations confidently while highlighting your skills to your network. When I was looking for an entry-level cyber role, it was those declarations of my interest to work in that space to a fellow intern and my supervisor at the time that created for me opportunities to intern in other departments within the same organization. As someone who was resetting and rebuilding my career while raising my children, I never took any opportunity for granted as long as it was serving me to reach my goals. I often felt like I had to work harder to prove myself so that folks could see me for my potential beyond their biases and stereotypes.

I can't stress enough the value of advocating for oneself, be it in negotiating your pay, or earning the respect of your peers, being proactive for opportunities, and being willing to take actions to increase your chances of reaching your goals and achieving success in this field.

4. Personal Branding - Amplifying Your Impact

As a Black woman in a white male-dominated industry, having a strong personal brand is key to advancing your career. But what exactly is a personal brand? Simply put, it's your unique identity and the way you market yourself to potential employers or clients. It conveys who you are, your values, and the value you bring to the table.

So, how do you build a personal brand in cyber? The journey starts with self-reflection and understanding your strengths and weaknesses. Then, it's all about consistency and authenticity in your online and offline presence, from your social media profiles to your resume and interactions with others. It helps with building your credibility and thought leadership inside and outside of your workplace.

I started building my personal brand in mid-2020 without even knowing what it was called. I started connecting with others in the industry on LinkedIn, gradually posting more about my experiences as a career changer, a mother, an immigrant, my grad school journey, as well as my journey to self-publishing my children's books. This consistency paid off, leading to being sought out for new job opportunities, speaking engagements, collaborations, media appearances, and more.

Public speaking was daunting for me, and I avoided it at any cost for a very long time. However, I know speaking in front of an audience is a valuable skill that can help to showcase expertise, raise awareness about important issues, and share your ideas. It was challenging, but I pushed past my comfort zone knowing the rewards of getting my message and ideas across. Whether it be through presenting at conferences, attending webinars, or speaking to the media, pushing the limits, and facing the fear of public speaking allowed me to be on a journey to build a strong personal brand. I not only landed but delivered my first TEDx talk this year to share my idea as a cyber advocate on empowering children on their online safety journey and cybersecurity. It allowed me to learn a ton in the process, push myself to share an idea worth spreading with the world and establish myself as a thought leader in the cybersecurity industry.

Building a personal brand takes time, so don't expect instant results. Start with one platform, such as LinkedIn, which is a great place to start building and engage meaningfully with others in your network. Remember to be true to yourself and highlight your unique experiences, skills, and personality as a Black woman in cybersecurity.

To learn more about building your brand in cybersecurity, check out my LinkedIn Learning Course on Cybersecurity Careers: Build Your Brand in Cybersecurity.

5. Problem Solving - Stepping Out of Your Comfort Zone

Continuous learning and stepping out of one's comfort zone are crucial in the constantly evolving field of cybersecurity. This isn't a field where you earn a degree and you are set and done. Staying up to date with the latest technologies, techniques, threats, and industry conversations is necessary to succeed in this industry. Moreover, challenging oneself to go beyond the familiar and embrace new opportunities is what sets the best apart from the rest.

One innovative way to demonstrate expertise in cyber and make an impact is by solving problems you witness in the industry. In today's digital age, it is especially important for the next generation to understand the importance of online safety and cybersecurity as a career. I recognized how younger generations were using the internet and how as parents, guardians, and educators we were doing little to protect our children or the children in our lives. It had been only six months since I self-taught myself and self-published my first children's book "Proud in Her Hijab" when I had the realization that I needed to do something about this. I saw this problem close to home when two of my children got hacked while gaming online more than once, and saw time and time again similar stories on parenting social media groups. Even though I was in the middle of a grad school program, a full-time job, and four kids getting schooled at home in the midst of the pandemic, I was compelled to shed light on the problem by publishing a children's book. "Oh, No... Hacked Again!", a multi-award-winning children's book that received an outstanding review from Kirkus review serves as a conversation starter for teaching children the importance of online safety. The book also sparks interest among young readers to consider cybersecurity as a career option in an inclusive manner portraying characters that look like me to pursue the field of cyber.

A year later, I published my third children's book "See Yourself in Cybersecurity" another Amazon #1 international bestseller and award-winner geared towards middle and high schoolers to inspire and encourage diverse children, teens, and youth to not only learn the various roles in the industry but also see themselves in cybersecurity.

Stepping out of my comfort zone, I combined my cyber expertise and motherhood experiences with storytelling, inspiring young readers to consider this industry which needs the expertise of the generations to come.

6. Leaning on Mentors & Allies

It can be challenging to navigate and succeed as an immigrant and career changer. However, having the support of mentors and those who gave you your first opportunity can make all the difference.

I never had a mentor back home or after I moved to the U.S. until mid-2020. I never knew or thought I needed any mentors. Mentors offer guidance and support in your professional journey, helping you overcome obstacles and reach your goals. They can also provide valuable insights and advice, connecting you with industry contacts and offering constructive feedback on your journey.

Having a mentor who believes in your abilities and is willing to invest time in your growth can provide a sense of belonging and validation, boosting your confidence and motivation. The potential mentor I randomly reached out to on LinkedIn after attending one webinar during the pandemic happened to be that person for me. He always made time, always believed in me, and never allowed me to doubt myself. He simply leads by doing and even when we aren't connecting, he is mentoring through his actions, and I am very grateful for his mentorship. I believe mentorship is a two-way street. You have to be intentional, be coachable, and be willing to put in the work.

Similarly, those who gave you your first chance to succeed in cyber play a crucial role in your journey. Whether it was a supportive manager, a coworker who encouraged you to pursue a career in the field, or a hiring manager who took a chance on you, they opened doors and provided the foundation for your success. I had a couple of those supportive supervisors when I was an intern who believed in my potential and advocated on my behalf, and I am grateful for them too.

It's important to acknowledge mentors and true allies, as they are instrumental in paving the way for future generations of Black women in cyber. Moreover, it's also crucial to pay it forward and become a mentor and advocate for other women in cyber. By offering your support and guidance, you can help close the gender gap and create a more inclusive and diverse industry for all. I try my best to volunteer, invest my time in educating the younger generation through school and library visits as time allows me. I mentored high school students, those who are looking to make entry to the field, as well as volunteering my time with a non-profit that is working to increase industry awareness and diversity in cyber, privacy, and STEM for women of color - Black Girls in Cyber.

Leaning on mentors and those who gave you your first chance to succeed in cyber can be the difference between struggle and success.

Securing cyber possibilities requires a combination of continuous education, strategic use of time, and the power to seize opportunities and advocate for yourself. Don't be afraid to take risks and push yourself beyond your comfort zone to achieve your goals - that's where growth happens.

Lean on the people who will lift you up, your support system, folks who will bring up your name in your absence. Be in spaces where you are celebrated, not tolerated. You already have what it takes to succeed and thrive in this lucrative and impactful industry.

Securing your Cyber Possibilities Worksheet

Answer the questions below to reflect on how you can apply the principles of securing your possibilities to your career in cyber.

- How can you prioritize education and self-development in your cyber career plan and make time for it?

- What are your current learning goals? How can you take advantage of the training and professional development opportunities currently available to you? Does your organization offer any training? What are the ways you could obtain knowledge whether formal or informal to achieve your career goals?

- How can you best utilize your time to achieve your goals? What strategies can you implement to prioritize tasks, stay focused, while avoiding burnout? Create a list of your current career goals and priorities.

- What steps can you take to prevent burnout and maintain your mental health?

- What is holding you back from seizing opportunities? How can you stay proactive, be open to new possibilities, and advance in this constantly evolving field?

- What steps can you take to advocate for yourself and advance your career?

- What is the one problem that you are looking to solve? What is your branded solution to that problem? Be clear about the problem that you try to solve in your industry, this further helps you establish yourself as an authority within the cyber industry.

- How can you make a name for yourself? Where do you share your achievements?

- How often can you commit to writing blog posts/articles to share your expert perspective on trending industry-related topics?

- What are the available opportunities for a Call for Papers to speak and attend events?

- Who are the individuals that you need in your life and career to be successful? A mentor or coach?

Develop your secure network of support. Write out your list and create a plan to further nurture those relationships.

Bonus - Share your insights and experiences with a fellow Black woman in cyber to inspire and support each other in achieving your career goals.

Securing possibilities requires intentional effort and commitment to growth. Apply these principles to your career in cyber to create opportunities for yourself and pave the way for other women of Color or Black women to succeed in the industry.

Zinet Kemal

Cloud Security Engineer | TEDx Speaker | 3 X Children's Book Author

Zinet Kemal, is an immigrant from Ethiopia, a mother of four, a career changer from the legal field, a multi-award-winning cybersecurity advocate, a TEDx speaker, LinkedIn Learning instructor, & 3 x published award-winning children's book author.

Zinet is a Georgia Tech University graduate with a M.S. degree in Cybersecurity. She earned a B.S. degree in Computer Science and LLB degree in Law. She currently works for a Fortune 500 organization as a Cloud Security Engineer and serves on a non-profit organization board, Black Girls in Cyber as a Community Outreach director.

Her children's books, "Proud in Her Hijab," champions girls' empowerment, and "Oh, No ... Hacked Again!" teaches children about the importance of online safety and sparks interest in young readers to consider cybersecurity as an exciting meaningful career option.

Her latest release 'See Yourself in Cybersecurity' an international Amazon #1 bestseller and award winner is a beacon for middle and high schoolers, illuminating the myriad cyber careers that await the next generation of trailblazers. Through her words, Zinet empowers young minds to envision themselves as the cyber heroes of tomorrow.

Zinet is the recipient of the 2023 Minneapolis/St. Paul Business Journal 40 under 40, the CS Hub Top 25 Cybersecurity Leader for 2024, the 2023 Ivan Allen Legacy Award from Graduate school, winner of the 2023 SANS Difference Makers Award Best Book of the Year, Women Who Code Applaud Her Awards in Security, 2022 SC media women in IT Security Cyber Advocate, CyberScoop Most Inspiring Up & Comer, 2021 Team Women's WaveMakers Award - Unchartered Territory.

She was featured on Good Morning America, 11Alive, BBC, Voice of America, Yahoo! News, Abc news, CBS Minnesota - WCCO. As well as a guest on a number of cyber podcasts.

Connect with Zinet:

LinkedIn - https://www.linkedin.com/in/zinetkemal

Website - https://www.zinetkemal.com/

CHAPTER 11

Pathway to Purpose - Daring To Disrupt Tradition

By: Dr. Diana B. Allen

"Those who disrupt their industries change consumer behavior, alter economies and transform lives" ~Anonymous

---

I have been disrupting my whole life; from the moment my mother thought she was having bad indigestion and was unexpectedly told by a doctor that I was in her womb tucked cozily behind an organ, to the day I earned a senior role in security at a Fortune 10 company. I am a first-generation Caribbean American woman with a large family filled with doctors, nurses and attorneys. As many people born to parents from non- US countries, careers in the medical arena or government are deemed the most coveted and stable. They sit on the phone with people from "back home" and boast about the fruit that their hard work and sacrifice manifested in their successful children. Sometime in elementary school, I confidently told my mother, a passionate and accomplished Registered Nurse, that I wanted to help people in a different way than being a doctor or nurse. Spoiler alert: while I am quite well versed in laws and regulations, I did not become a lawyer. I am a successful cyber professional. To add a little spice to the mix, I choose not to engineer or write code!

I have had some very tough career lessons - some of which have been straight up traumatic. But those experiences fostered a tenacity and resilience in me that has helped me be a better cyber professional and stronger leader that is known for being biased towards action. Now decades later, when faced with adversity or an unfamiliar challenge I ask myself "How do I get to 'yes'?" and "What is another way to look at this to make this happen or not?" Throughout my career, I have picked up *nuggets* of wisdom along the way- some I earned myself and some were gifted to me. In all instances, I have gathered them and held them close to my heart because the insight they have provided are pure *gold.* So if you have a yearning to disrupt what others have tried to lay out for you and delve into the tech and security world - pull up a seat, grab a cup of tea and read on while I share a few precious *Golden Nuggets* about how I have been challenging the status quo of what it looks and sounds like to work in technology.

My educational background in information security, my love for books and organizational leadership, coupled with my strong writing skills have enabled me to combine my passions and talents to walk in my purpose and disrupt meaningfully. My journey to successfully working for some of the largest organizations in the world did not come easy nor was it linear. My cyber career started out in Consulting. Specifically, I was an IT Auditor. I supported my clients by developing deep expertise in the laws, regulations and mandates impacting IT systems. I was able to effectively dissect relevant regulations for my clients prior to them undergoing review from regulatory agencies. I helped them update critical documentation and draft strategic plans of action to maintain the integrity of their security environments. I elevated in my career because I was able to ideate with the engineers, administrators and developers while also being able to translate technical jargon to non-technical people and keep them engaged in efforts. Remember that I mentioned earlier that I was a strong writer with a love for people? Those attributes help me ensure that my interactions with others are memorable in a positive way. I chose to re-define success in a way that aligned with my values, my innate desire to make significant impacts and achieve excellence.

The first *Golden Nugget* and piece of advice to you is to embrace the fact that you are a mosaic. We are a product of our experiences and exposure. Your personal experiences are what make you a unique value-add and empowers you to leave an indelible mark on those who you encounter. I will never forget attending a client meeting with a senior leader–an older white male as a relatively new manager in the company. We arrived to the conference room a bit early to get settled in and make sure we were prepared. The client, a Black woman, came in and joined us in the room shortly before the meeting was to start. She sparked a conversation with me about how much she loved my hairstyle (a twist out) and asked me for some tips on mirroring the style. The senior leader sat there with his short, straight hair unable to add to the conversation but nodded along, smiled and observed the interaction. The meeting went extremely well, but the rapport built with that particular client lasted well beyond that experience and garnered us increased business. That day, the senior leader was able to witness a fond exchange that was heartfelt and uncensored. Later on I realized that my ability to lean into the various aspects of my authentic self brings a prodigious competitive advantage. I encourage you to embrace all of your different facets and the "hats" which make you who you are because you do not know which one will be needed that will resonate with the person or people you are trying to engage, influence or lead.

Every success, every win, every stumble, every tear, every encounter, every dream fulfilled, every almost, every miss, every love, every disappointment, every laugh, every memorable experience- no matter how big or small- is a piece of the mosaic of you. Each experience helped and continues to help to shape you as a professional and a leader. Take a moment to collect the pieces that make you uniquely you and I wholeheartedly believe you will see a priceless masterpiece come into form.

Now, I understand you may be thinking that it's easier said than done–especially since I work in the industry and you may also be wondering, have there been times in which

I got scared creating the masterpiece? Since we are building a friendship here, I will give you the honest answer, YES! I still get scared sometimes, but it happens less and less as I have grown in my career.

My second *Golden Nugget* for you is to understand that disruption can be extremely scary, but be assiduous and use the fear as your fuel. Determine your path and go for it with your knees shaking, teeth chattering, and stomach trembling because you will be SO proud of yourself when you arrive.

A huge disruption for me was when I turned 18 and did not go down the path of being a medical doctor or lawyer. Instead, I chose to move to Washington, DC to attend Howard University and major in Business with a concentration in Information Systems and Analysis. My family had no real understanding of computers, cyber, nor perspective on its future impact on the economy, but the digital age was booming. I was the family anomaly and that was scary. Midway through my college matriculation I realized that I cared more about management, enabling strong business outcomes and the motivations behind people's behavior within the organization than I did about database management. My parents encouraged me (in the kind yet threatening way that only parents can) to stay on course to finish my degree. When I graduated, I sought to pivot my path a bit to learn more about business and how technology can realize business objectives. Venturing to pivot in this way when my peers were joining companies in standard roles for new grads such as Business Systems Analysts was a disruption in its own right. The challenge was, I had a hard time identifying a role that encompassed what I was after as a career starting point. So I made the decision to challenge tradition again.

My very first job out of undergrad, before I entered into consulting was at a bank. That's right, I was a personal banker. I took the role because I did not want a traditional "tech" job, the salary was decent and I was excited to interact with people even though I was very shy. Hard to believe, I know - but it's the truth. I told you earlier that my path was not linear. This goes to confirm that what you do is a by-product of who you are not the other way around. I did get several valuable take-aways out of that personal banking role which I carry with me until this day.

I learned how to talk to people who I did not know and how to successfully build trust and rapport with them quickly. This proved very handy when I had to meet new clients, customers and team members. Additionally, I learned to sell. This skill was particularly helpful as I have elevated into more senior-client facing roles and been charged with growing the business. I learned about protecting customer data, physical security, and other security principles. Lastly, I got my first cyber job from that role. One of my banking clients was a leader at a small minority-owned consulting firm, he learned of my educational background, liked my customer service skills, and thought I would be a great asset to the organization. I interviewed with his company and got the position.

A few years later, after finishing my MBA in Management, I landed a Senior role at a Big 4 Consulting firm. The rumors about the fast paced, competitive nature of the industry were daunting to say the least. I was riddled with thoughts such as "What if I don't succeed?" "How will I maintain my quality of life and feel fulfilled?" I had no answer to those questions or action plan but I took the job anyway. When I got there, I was nervous and sometimes scared. Some things that helped me stand out then and continue to be advantageous to me now are pieces of my mosaic: I have excellent problem-solving skills, I am detail-oriented, remain calm under pressure and people needed those skills. Through my tenure there, I was extremely blessed to find amazing mentors and sponsors, who I now consider friends, who showed me the ropes, gave me room to be inquisitive and opportunities to thrive.

My third *Golden Nugget* for you if you are willing to disrupt tradition to achieve success is to identify your vision and be creative in times of challenge. Adversity will come whether you are ready or not so have courage when it does. Be courageous when using your voice, sharing your ideas and identifying solutions. Disruption requires courage and innovation requires disruption. I encourage you to show up how you want to be seen, lean into fear, when it makes sense, and let it fuel you to reposition yourself for your best future. Remember, you are a mosaic and your career path is uniquely yours.

My fourth *Golden Nugget* for you is to think of your career journey as a collage. Identify people or roles that have elements of what you desire or need in a career and add that to your collage. There may be times when you are the "only" of some intersectionality within a particular space. Lean into it - highlight it as a competitive advantage and an asset, not a liability. For areas unchartered, where you can not find a template, map out a vision to get there and proceed until apprehended! Recognize that being the "first" or "only" is a form of productive disruption. Diversity of thought, gender, experiences, socio-economic backgrounds, and capabilities among the leaders of organizations was documented by McKinsey & Company, Inc.[7] as a key factor to the realization of increased profitability by almost fifty percent.

Let me take a moment to be abundantly clear, your presence alone is not the value-add. Please do not fall into the trap of believing that your ability to deliver, possession of charm or "magic" alone entitles you to access to the rooms with influential leaders. Your competitive advantage comes from gathering the knowledge, skills, abilities, and experiences to empower you to excel, have a valuable and relevant point of view, and possess subject matter authority in the rooms you occupy in ADDITION TO your lived experiences. You do not simply need a "seat in the room", you need to thrive from the second that you walk into it!

My last *Golden Nugget* for you is for you to remember that you do not have to go after it alone. You need allies and mentors in your career. More importantly, you need sponsors. Sponsors are the people who advocate on your behalf for the big career opportunities, promotions and

---

[7] Dixon-Fyle, S., Dolan, K., Hunt, V., & Prince, S. (2020). Diversity wins: how inclusion matters. McKinsey & Company. Inc.: London, UK.

raises in the rooms where you are not present. Women in tech - especially women of color- are often under sponsored and over mentored. When you get a sponsor, make sure you consistently perform and strive for excellence. Afterall, they are putting their political capital on the line behind your ability to execute. Also, make sure to have a tribe, a circle or a squad of people with whom you can connect and who understand what you do (somewhat), your goals, and your talents. These people will be priceless along your career journey. They will help you stay focused, remind you of your abilities, and ideally uplift you when you get tired or fearful. For me, they are affectionately referred to as "my crew". My crew keeps me laughing, they show up when I need them, and they help me regroup as necessary when the crown of ambition gets too heavy. Remember, the best ideas won't come when you're worn out or tired.

Do not forget your family. Regardless of whether it's the family you were born into or one you selected and created for yourself, those people should allow you the space to be you and shine. Your ability to relax and connect with others along your career journey will help you identify the best ways to meaningfully disrupt.

In conclusion, I shared these *Golden Nuggets* to help you chart your course to recognizing your beautiful mosaic faster than I did. There were times early in my career where I felt that other people had insights that I did not. The feeling was palpable, but I could not simply go find the information myself because it is extremely hard to put your finger on something when you don't know what you do not know. If you have ever felt that way then this chapter was for you.

For those of you who did not have family ties to business leaders, role models or cyber champions to guide you when you decided to pursue a cyber career, lean into the discomfort of disrupting the norm. There is nothing wrong with honoring your legacy and starting new traditions. Channel your courage and remain creative as you navigate great challenges, innovate and grow.

Last but not least, take care of yourself, eat great food, rest, and recharge your mind. Find people to share love and laughter with because it makes this journey a whole lot more bearable and worthwhile. I challenge you to choose disruption over tradition, from my own personal experience I can attest - your life will never be the same.

Dr. Diana B. Allen

Senior Technology Program Manager | Google

Dr. Diana B. Allen is a highly sought-after global speaker renowned for her profound insights into leadership and technology. With a distinguished doctorate in organizational leadership, her groundbreaking research focused on "Empowerment & the Career Sponsorship of Women in STEM."

As a leading figure in the cyber industry, Diana currently spearheads risk and program management activities for hybrid cloud endeavors at Google in addition to teaching college students as an adjunct professor. Her expertise extends across multiple domains, including FinTech and consulting with some of the world's largest companies.

Beyond her professional accomplishments, Diana is equally dedicated to philanthropic endeavors. She champions causes close to her heart, supporting initiatives that promote education and equality in STEM fields. In her spare time, Diana finds joy in reading, maintaining her fitness, and cherishing moments with her friends and family.

Diana's passion lies in the comprehensive growth of individuals. She brings this to life through coaching, mentoring, and nurturing the next generation of STEM professionals. Her hands-on experience also encompasses designing and facilitating courses dedicated to enhancing professional skills, cultivating positive cultures and fostering personal leadership development to yield impactful business outcomes.

Diana's mission is clear: to empower and inspire, bridging the gap between technology, leadership, and personal growth.

Connect with Diana:

https://www.linkedin.com/in/dianaballen13/

|www.dianaballen.com

CHAPTER 12

A Patient Pursuit of Purpose

By: Tashya Denose

"So what is my purpose?" I cried loud and ugly with a runny nose, a tear-stained beat face, and clumpy lashes, longing for a response as I looked into my best friend's eyes. That day, I was completely broken; standing in the middle of a hotel room in downtown Atlanta, Georgia. I was desperate and confused, but dressed impeccably in the epitome of Y2K fashion—a wide silver belt, check; matching peep-toe shoes, check; and the large statement necklace, which was the star of the show, check. The spirals in my ponytail were still bouncing, yet I was so distraught because we had sat outside on the nasty sidewalk in front of Club 112 for over 24 hours straight, waiting for an opportunity to become the next host on BET's *106 and Park*. In my mind, my future was undoubtedly going to consist of television appearances draped in high fashion. I was locked in, and there would be no deviations from the course. Fast forward almost twenty years, and that young girl has taken every back road and highway to find herself, and now in a moment of full reflection. I know I am living my purpose and I've built a foundation upon the most meaningful aspects of my life's journey.

This path to discovering myself was slightly arduous. Much like many of my peers, I was told that I was born with two strikes against me. As a Black woman, I represent two marginalized groups and the flawed societal construct that perpetuates the idea that Black women are always one bad swing away from losing at this game of life. Not to mention the fact that my voice carries, my nails are long, shiny, and distracting, and my hair is set to change with the swings of my mood. These physical attributes that many would discredit and call frivolous are what sustain my "main character." I made a vow to myself that those attributes would never take a backseat during my journey and I would remain authentically me.

I often found myself confused and second-guessing whether I belonged in each role. I had numerous starring roles as a bank teller, a retail store merchandising manager, an office administrator, and even a stand-up comedian. I knew my purpose was laced with connecting with people, using my oratory skills, and a constant yearning to learn new things. What I didn't know when I started down that path was that each step would teach me a new skill that future me would be thankful for. As a bank teller, I learned the importance of people's privacy, what they needed to protect, and what was important to them. As a manager in the fashion industry, I learned about customer service, how to connect with people, and how important it was to see where another person was coming from in order to communicate effectively. As an office administrator, I learned the importance of understanding what was important to the business and how to ensure the mission was being accomplished. And, lastly, as a comedian, I learned that we're all humans, and no matter what background we come from, we should all be connecting through that common thread and doing our best to enjoy life. As I was collecting soft skills and layering them together, I found that I was laying a foundation for new opportunities to build upon. So, as my father says, I was preparing myself for the opportunity before it presented itself.

That opportunity came in the form of an executive assistant position at the Pentagon for the Security Director of the Information Technology Agency. This moment came along with several pivotal moments for my career. The first was salary negotiations. At this time, I was making less than $45,000 a year to manage a small engineering office. When my negotiations began for my fancy new administration position, my mother urged me to ask for $65,000. I was too shocked to argue with her. I had to take a moment to think. Why did this number scare me? Why did I feel like I was a fraud and they would see right through me? She pushed, "Ask them, and all they can say is no," she chanted to me all morning as I prepared to have the last conversation with the recruiter. Finally, on the call, with wide eyes and a fast-beating heart, I spat out the words vehemently, "I would like $65,000 plus benefits." The way the recruiter responded with ease, as I look back, I know I probably could've asked for more, but it was more than enough to commence my amazing journey.

Walking down the sterile halls of the Pentagon basement, I thought to myself, "Wow, I really made it." I couldn't believe it. As an Air Force brat the significance of the Pentagon had been etched into my mind. This was the pinnacle of military excellence. I knew my parents were proud. On my breaks, I would venture to the floors where the historical plaques and medals were displayed and think, "How in the hell did they let me through the doors?" I would chuckle and follow up with, "Well, it's too late, I'm in here now!"

My organization had the daunting mission of operating and securing all of the major Pentagon networks and the systems connected to them. My mission was to keep the Security Director's calendar and communications on track. The job was high-paced and exciting, and the problems that we were solving were dynamic. I had never been a part of something like this. My brain was stimulated, and I yearned for more. Yet, each day was filled with the dichotomy of solving new technological obstacles in a room full of old white men. The problems weren't the only thing new in the room; I was also the complete opposite. I was steadfast in keeping my main character's energy, and I had the dress code to match. Each time I entered the room, everyone heard the click-clack of my heels and a view of my sleek midi skirts and colorful frilly button-up tops. I refused to minimize myself to fit in a room of bald heads and an ill-fitting navy suit.

Determined to stand out for more than my appearance, I pushed myself to master the inner workings of our organization. As I took notes in the meetings, I focused on each player, their perspective, and how they supported the mission while assessing how the executive always obtained the outcome he desired. Once I had the basics down, I took it a step further and began to research the technical aspects of all the information surrounding me. I found myself getting comfortable speaking on topics and actually having opinions. My leader took notice. Our clinical conversations about his calendar transformed into strategic discussions on how I thought his meetings would go and what approach he should take.

Six months went by in the blink of an eye. As I became embedded in the organization, I focused my time on building relationships with people who supported my growth. There was plenty of opposition around me from those who didn't like that I was evolving into more than an assistant. I welcomed the adversity with a wide grin and poppin' lip gloss. My director was my biggest ally. He, too, received backlash for supporting my advancement but ignored it and kept pushing me forward. One day, he pulled me into his office and sat me down. He stated curiously, "You really get what's going on around here, don't you?" I laughed and responded in the most assertive tone, "Why, yes, sir, I do." He came back with, "Well, I think you should get training." And that was it; I was to be formally introduced to the world of cyber.

The paperwork was signed, and I was on my way to CompTIA boot camp. I went hard out of the gate and chose the three foundational certifications: A+ for hardware basics, Network+ for network configuration, and Security+ to provide me with the qualifications to officially begin my career in IT security. I had never been more focused. I felt as if there was no turning back. This was the point in my life where I felt God's favor, and I knew if I pushed forward, there would be a generous return. I studied, passed all three exams, and returned to work empowered with authority to support my advancement.

In the following months, I found and trained my replacement and began to dive into my newly found purpose. I could not define it as the job but more so how I felt about myself in it. For so long I had searched for my meaning in life and settled on it being here to do one or two particular things. In this new role, I saw that my purpose was more than that; it was to fulfill my potential and become comfortable utilizing all parts of me. Being a young Black woman in the Pentagon and weighing in on how to solve complex problems in a room filled with what one could call my opposition is an impact I didn't know I could make. I settled into who I was becoming. My niche was being able to communicate technical solutions to non-technical stakeholders.

My beginnings as an Information Systems Security Officer were filled with odd projects that no one had the energy to solve. My strategy was to dress the ugly babies well enough to compete in pageants. Meaning I would take full ownership of the problem no one wanted, not only solve it but also streamline the process with an aligned strategy so it would never be an issue again. Eventually, these ugly babies grew into cute toddlers that everyone wanted to play with. Problems became programs with allotted resources, and this gave me notoriety in the organization.

This was also the time in my life when I gained another layer of mental toughness. As a great philosopher once said, "If you ain't got no haters, you ain't poppin'!" Well, I was "poppin" because the hate was constantly swarming around me, and at times it was suffocating. I was fighting the people's perception of authority, which was a white male. Each time I entered a conference room, I armed myself with an impenetrable veil of self-confidence, knowing that I was going into the battlefield of mental warfare. Everything was going to be challenged, and everything I said was going to be discredited, yet preparation has always beat arrogance. My external appearance was stealth; I never showed my hand because, on the inside, there were times I was overwhelmed with self-doubt. At the time, I didn't know it had a name—imposter syndrome. The psychological occurrence in which an individual doubts their skills, talents, or accomplishments and has a persistently internalized fear of being exposed as a fraud. I didn't know it was normal, but I did know that I wasn't going to let it slow me down. I was in my Maya Angelou, "Still I Rise," era, and the constant prevalence of opposition solidified my belief that I was in the right place. Defying the idea of what was normal in this space was devoid of purpose.

My drive, ability to accept and learn from criticism, plus an unwavering belief that God had me enabled me to get promoted and expand my expertise from system security to audit readiness and then to vulnerability management. After four years of evolution at the Pentagon, it was time to go on a new adventure. I went on to the Secret Service, the Intelligence Community, then the public sector at Capital One, Google, and now, Meta. Within all these positions, there is still one glaring similarity: I am still one of the only Black women in the room. Yet, I have found my place, paving the way for that to change.

Are you looking to make a change? Are you feeling your way through life, looking for purpose? Well, know that you are meant to leave an imprint on the world. Your mere presence is evidence that God is real and with you. My first piece of advice is to step back, look at all the challenges you have already overcome in life, and give yourself some grace. I've found that those of us striving to be better tend to be too hard on ourselves, especially Black women. As soldiers in the battle against mediocrity, we are always forcing ourselves to level up. I just want to say, "Sis, you are on the right path; each step is laid out for you to excel in your divine purpose."

To ease your mind on your journey, I would like to provide you with the framework that helped me. There are three themes that were prevalent on my path. First, I found my tribe. Then, I was my biggest cheerleader. Lastly, I learned to "lean not unto my own understanding."

The revamping of my social circle was one of the painful challenges that I had to endure. It took a while for me to grasp that not everyone is meant to level up with you for various reasons: some have their own path that is not aligned with yours; some are not prepared to be on your path at this particular juncture; and some are jealous of your favor and it's just time to let them go. Once I realized that it was okay to build new relationships, I attracted my dream team. My star player was my ally and sponsor, who believed in me enough to give me a chance. Another included a coworker turned friend who was so set on us Black women succeeding that she shared her salary and tips for negotiating. She taught me how to influence recruiters to obtain the best offer. Another was my "cert buddy," a friend who pushed me to continue to get trained and certified. Most importantly, my husband aka My Person, the one I could be vulnerable with. He is supportive and reminds me to take my time and believe in myself. You have people waiting to do the same for you. Once you commit yourself to change, remember that this includes the people you surround yourself with.

"I AM HER!" "Yes, I am she!" is a constant theme song running in the back of my mind. Because if I'm not playing it for myself, who's going to play it for me? You have to give yourself props. You have to take time to celebrate your wins with yourself. Many times, we are looking for validation from the outside. Trust me, I am no different, but I discovered that when I began to pat myself on the back first without the cheers from others, it meant more. I saw my own light, which empowered me to protect it. Once you trust your greatness, you are less likely to let those who are dealing with their own issues dim it.

The most important thing is to pay your dues to the architect of your life, God. I believe we are a piece of the divine. The vastness of this universe created us. How could the one who allows planes to defy gravity and paints the sky with the rising sun each morning steer me wrong? I am still learning but I found that the more I trust God has ordered my steps, I find the path more beautiful. Therefore, I leave you with this: "You are amazing; every choice you've made has led you to this moment." Have faith and know that the past version of you is proud, and the future version of you is thanking you for the decisions you are making today.

Tashya Denose

Sr Security Program Manager | Meta Reality Labs

Tashya Denose isn't just a cyber professional; she's a passionate advocate with a distinct mission. Her focus is on empowering women in the industry and redefining the cyber landscape through a lens of emotional intelligence. As a committed board member of Black Girls In Cyber, she drives positive change by providing Black women with the resources they need to transition into cyber and privacy roles, aiming to uplift their socioeconomic status.

Adding to her impactful initiatives, Tashya hosts a thought-provoking podcast titled "Do We Belong Here." Through this podcast, she delves into the human aspects of cyber, with a special focus on diversity. Produced in collaboration with Cyber Florida, the podcast paints a vivid picture of the multifaceted world of cyber, revealing its deeply human nuances.

Tashya's diverse background spans from offering her expertise in vulnerability management, governance, risk, and compliance to the US Department of Defense, US Secret Service, and the Intelligence community, to holding key roles at renowned institutions such as Capital One, Google, and now, Meta's Reality Labs.

In a sector largely defined by technology, Tashya Denose emerges as a transformative figure, accentuating the vital role of emotional intelligence and empathy in cyber. Her commitment to elevating the voices of underrepresented groups and her skill in bridging the technical-human divide mark her as a genuine pioneer in her field.

CHAPTER 13

"I Transformed My Tests into My Testimonies"

By: Juliet U Okafor, JD

---

*"They tried to bury me, but they didn't know I
was a mustard seed."*

~Adapted from the poet, Dinos Christianopoulos

I started my career in cyber by replying to a suspicious post on Craigslist. How ironic? I responded to a mysterious "Account Executive" job post on the platform. At the time, I was so desperate for employment, I searched every job board I could find. I had no idea that Craigslist, a local public square, would be where I found my purpose. As a Security Culture trailblazer, I truly believe that the path to my success will always be found by pursuing the roads least traveled.

Let me take you back to how I, an attorney and CEO, managed to arrive there. In March of 2013, I, along with 15 other salespeople was laid off by a market research firm in Washington, DC. My boss had been taken into a meeting and told that she should quit and anyone that she'd hired would also be let go. Shortly thereafter, many of us were called into a conference room and given the bad news: We were all being let go that day. And – since none of us had been in the role more than six months, we would receive no more than two weeks severance pay. I was not at all prepared for this turn of events. My world felt as though it were caving in around me.

I went home that night and told my very unsupportive and abusive ex-husband, in front of my in-laws that I had been laid off. He looked at me and then looked at them. Then he laughed. You can tell when a laugh is designed to harm. Even today, when I have a bad day, lose a deal, or miss a deadline, I hear that deep-throated, hearty, belly-tickling laugh that my ex-husband released in front of his family, and which was designed to humiliate me. There was no need to kick me, I was down – bad.

The following May, when I decided to keep accepting unemployment, receiving WIC from the State of Maryland,

and patiently awaiting the birth of my daughter was when I gave in to the reality of my situation. It was then that the emotional and mental toll that I was putting on myself was released. One morning, while cleaning the kitchen and when the baby was napping, I fell to my knees. I could hear God. I listened. I would be directed. This was but a short test. But I knew with everything in me, that the place in which I'd found myself would not be where I would reside long. God had other plans for me. So, I had to hold fast and have faith that better days would come.

I would classify myself as more of a spiritual person than a religious one. But there were pivotal times in my life when it was time to transition, and I could hear the voice to comfort and lead me. One day, I heard the voice, kneeled, and prayed to God, "Please God, I want to find a job in an industry that is growing. I promise if I find a job in a high-growth industry, I will never look back. I will get to the top of that industry and help other women and disadvantaged people like me." A promise made is a promise never broken.

Upon starting my new role in cyber as an Account Executive for a Managed Services Provider, I decided to build a new, personal brand. Jules, unlike Juliet, was confident, passionate, and on an individual mission to save herself, by helping and serving others in, across, and through the cyber industry. Everyone still calls me Jules. Juliet no longer feels like who I am. To me, she represented the people-pleasing, co-dependent, validation-seeking perfectionist daughter, sister, and wife I no longer wanted to be.

I received my Master's degree in Public Communications and Media Studies at Fordham University in 2003, from the Graduate School of Arts and Sciences. Fordham's mission is based on the principle of, "cura personalis"[1] which is an Ignatian-Jesuit characteristic and Latin for "care for the whole person." Cura personalis comes down to the respect for all that makes up everyone. Learning is as important as a good diet. We pray, learn, and eat healthy as ways to glorify God and care for our entire selves. [2]

I was never taught to care for myself. I have been raised to believe my salvation was intricately tied to the people I helped and how society viewed me. I was trained that my value was based on how good a wife or mother I would be in a home I built with my husband. So, you can only imagine how easy it was to separate myself from my name, Juliet Okafor Ebo, the name I had in the Nigerian community. I chose to become Jules Okafor. It was important to shed that name and previous skin to survive. I wanted to leave behind the broken girl who I had been and step into the woman God had destined that I would become.

Changing my name alone didn't change my life. All the time I was building this amazing career, I was hiding my deepest secrets. Juliet Okafor Ebo was sexually abused as a child, by her babysitter's husband when she was only 8 years old. I was abused and sent back into the home because my mother had no other choice of babysitters she could afford. I told my truth, and it was ignored. I buried that pain for many years.

Vowing to never let any man prey on my weakness and taking as much time as possible to remarry after my first marriage failed, I married a Nigerian man. He was the father of my two daughters. His family loved my family. But he was physically, mentally, spiritually and emotionally abusive. I stayed in a marriage where my successes were met with the silent treatment. I was scorned for promotions. I was envied for bonuses, and I was assaulted for any ascension. I thought my husband hated me healing despite him, not because of him. He tried everything he could to break me. I was his whipping horse and yet, I would not cease fighting. I fought to persist and exist – until I asked him to leave my house in 2018. One of the hardest decisions I ever had to make.

No one can tell you the path to your healing. No one shares how dark it can get before you see a glimmer of light. I look back now, and I was buried. This man had finally buried me under the weight of my own pain. I questioned whether even God could find me in this utter darkness. If I was honest, I didn't want him to find me. I wanted him to take me from this pain. I wanted God to deliver me to heaven or hell. I just could not stay on this earth. I absolutely wanted to die. I owe my life today to God and my daughters. They saved me from myself.

I ask everyone to check on the strong people. 2018 was the year I just really could not handle one more thing. I didn't know how to ask for help. I didn't have the ability to tell people my story. So, I kicked him out of the house on a Sunday night and went back to work on Monday. I never stopped working. I was dying inside on my personal side, but professionally I began to soar.

Cura personalis dictates we care for the whole human. Juliet Okafor Ebo has not been a whole human adult. I didn't care for that imperfect part of my life, so I shunned her and ran from her. If I focused on what was good and ignored the pain, I could just about survive the trauma and lean into the future. This is taught to women in all countries and cultures. We are taught to exist – to survive. Rarely are we taught to thrive. Thriving would require that I integrate all parts of myself – even the painful and less-than-perfect parts. I am still healing; the journey doesn't stop. I can see that by turning my back on my past for so long because I didn't want to address it, I kept putting my future in jeopardy.

I start with my personal story because there are so many women who may not have the same story but can find elements of their own stories in my life story. I know today that my first job in cyber saved my life. It saved my daughters and helped me to find my purpose. Now, as CEO & Founder of RevolutionCyber, I have a unique opportunity to create systemic lifelines and livelihoods for a generation of women who don't yet know the beautiful opportunities for wealth, career, and personal growth that exist within Cyber. My company, RevolutionCyber, was founded in 2019. Today, it's the first and only "Security Culture as-a-Service" firm. The topic of Security Culture sits at the intersection of Governance, Security Operations, Organizational Culture & DEI.

The future of cyber is quintessentially human. It is by tapping into Black women's deep humanity that we will lead the industry into the future. I built my business out of deep pain and developed my purpose. As CEO & Founder of "RevolutionCyber", I am on a mission to create and scale career and business access and opportunities for people from underrepresented groups.

*According to a study by IBM, human error is the main cause of 95% of cyber breaches…if human error was somehow eliminated entirely, 19 out of 20 cyber breaches may not have taken place at all! The current approach which utilizes Security Awareness technology and inexperienced awareness analysts is not working.

The truth is:

- Technology alone cannot address the human element. A complex problem such as human behavior requires a dedicated, cross-functional team of experts across behavioral science, psychology, education, design, and security to lead change and drive transformation.

- The threats grow ever more dynamic, targeted, and sophisticated. Therefore, a culture of continuous learning and improvement must remain at the center of any proposed solution, process, or technology.

General security awareness and phishing simulations are the flawed answer to yesterday's threats. Security Awareness programs in their current form began in 2014. We are still using old solutions to fight new battles. This means that the people who can solve today's challenges may not work in the industry yet. It also means that there is an opportunity to create the next generation of security culture experts from non-traditional fields who merely show high analytical ability, empathy, and a passion for helping people.

RevolutionCyber is a high-touch, security transformation consulting firm backed by the RCQx Platform, an all-in-one security culture & communication platform that automates, scales, and embeds security and privacy into the fabric of an enterprise. Using proven culture maturity models, coaching, and UX design content and templates, security leaders can create a positive connection between employee security performance metrics and business outcomes.

RevolutionCyber has transformed over sixty end-to-end enterprise-wide security awareness and culture programs, and each one was tailored to the unique risks, goals, and needs of the client organization. Our programs are run by senior-level security culture program managers, paired with apprentices and interns who receive up to six months of direct training before being certified as a Security Culture Coach. As a part of our program, apprentices can be considered for employment at RevolutionCyber or begin the process to seek a full-time entry-level role at another employer.

==

I envision the future of a direct pipeline between historically Black universities (HBCUs), NASA-designated university-level cyber schools of excellence, and apprenticeships at RevolutionCyber for Black and Brown students to become certified apprentices, interns, and franchise owners. In 2021, I began the process to begin franchising the business to enable it to be scaled to allow others who wished to follow my path to build their own businesses, with minimum initial investment, sales leads from day one, and the systems and processes outlined that they could use to grow their own companies to over $1M annual recurring revenue in two years! I am still on that journey, because it is possible, as I have done it, so can so many others. There is a way to scale this business, to help build other Security Leaders, who can make their own success, in their own way, without going into federal government contracting. This is no longer my dream. It is a reality that I continue to build towards every single day.

Today there is a much clearer understanding of the profound need for significant investment into the next generation of security professionals. They will come to the industry bringing much-needed business skills like law, teaching, change management, empathy, education, influence, servant leadership, writing, presentation, diplomacy, and communication. This modern workforce will also reflect the diversity of our collective experiences. And in doing so – a wonderful space is created for Black and Brown women to lead in the future of Cyber.

I truly believe the future of cyber is quintessentially human. It is by tapping into a Black Woman's deepest connection to humanity that will push the industry into its brilliant future." Yet, it will require that Black and Brown women build a network of White, Male allies that act as sponsors and identify hidden areas of opportunity. It may also require that "we stoop to conquer." The goal for the next generation of women should be to volunteer, engage, and seek out direct learning experiences for a period, which could within a year ensure a full pivot into their desired role. It is a journey – a sometimes painful lesson – but it has paid untold dividends for me when I did it so many years ago. In 2015, I increased my salary four times over by accepting a large pay cut, proving myself, and then taking a VP role within a year of starting as an Account Executive the year before. This is much harder to do today, but it isn't impossible. I strongly recommend women explore entry-level roles, gain experience, learn, network, and seek opportunities to rise whether inside or outside the organization.

According to an article published by JP Morgan, Black women are the fastest-growing demographic of entrepreneurs in the U.S., with nearly 2.7 million businesses nationwide. Despite our growing presence in entrepreneurship, we continue to face disproportionate financial headwinds in attracting business capital and funding. Like many women, I began RevolutionCyber with my personal savings, which I made as the SVP of Security Solutions for Fortress Information Security. Since then, it has grown into a boutique culture transformation consultancy, with clients from the Fortune 500 to small non-profit organizations.

I believe it is my mission to help other Black women start, scale, and run successful security consulting firms and SaaS companies. Today, my goal is to make RevolutionCyber the first security "Unicorn" (Company valued at $1 billion) led by a Black, Female Founder. Using the lessons I have learned in building my business, backed by my proven security culture methodology and 20+ years of sales and business experience, I want to build wealth and a legacy of Black Female Founders who will make their own way and force change in the faces we see as representative of cyber. I would love to meet, teach, and mentor Black and Brown women who have the desire, discipline, and dedication to start on this beautiful journey alongside RevolutionCyber! We will change lives. More importantly, you become the change you wish to see.

Juliet U Okafor, JD

Chief Executive Officer & Founder | RevolutionCyber

Juliet "Jules" Okafor, JD, is a remarkable force in the world of law, cyber, and gender equality. With a passion for justice, a dedication to her family, and an unwavering commitment to the advancement of women in the cyber field, Jules has emerged as a leading voice in the Security Culture, Privacy and DevSecOps domains.

Career Highlights:

Jules' journey into the world of cyber began with a deep-rooted desire to champion the rights of the underserved and underrepresented. Armed with a Juris Doctorate degree, she embarked on a career that would eventually lead her to tackle some of the most pressing cyber issues of our time.

As a mentor and coach, Jules has tirelessly fought for justice, advocating for those who need it most. Her business acumen and fierce determination have earned her a reputation as a formidable speaker, and security culture trailblazer across the world.

Recognizing the critical importance of cyber in our increasingly digital world, Jules set her sights on a new mission: to bridge the gender gap in this field. She co-founded RevolutionCyber, a groundbreaking cyber company that has become a beacon of empowerment for a diverse, non-traditional workforce seeking to enter the areas of governance, risk, and security culture transformation. Under her leadership, RevolutionCyber, the first "Security Culture as- a - Service" consultancy firm, has not only thrived but has also become a symbol of diversity and inclusion in a traditionally male-dominated industry.

Jules is a CHIEF member, Forbes Business Council member, and a member of the Security Tinkerers. She is also a member of the Dean's Advisory Board at the

Fordham University Graduate School of Arts and Science Program and Strategic Advisory Board Member for the Northeastern Illinois University and Dublin Youth Association in Dublin, OH. In addition, she is a highly sought-after, paid speaker. and has been a featured speaker/panelist at RSA, BlackHat, SANS Leadership Institute, and The Diana Initiative. She also has been featured or quoted in several information security and business publications.

Advocacy and Congressional Testimony:

Jules' commitment to racial and gender diversity in cyber is not confined to the boardroom. She has taken her advocacy to the highest levels of government, testifying at the invitation of Ranking Member, Congressman Bennie Thompson, before the Committee on Homeland Security about the urgent need to attract more minorities into cyber roles. Her compelling testimony highlighted the economic and security benefits of a more diverse cyber workforce.

Balancing Act:

Beyond her professional achievements, Jules is a devoted mother of two amazing young girls, proving that it is possible to excel in both career and family life. Her ability to balance the demands of a thriving cyber company, board membership, and motherhood is a testament to her unwavering determination and commitment to leading by example.

In all her endeavors, Jules Okafor, JD stands as a shining example of a modern leader, advocating for people-centric security, racial/gender equality, and our secure digital future. Her legacy will be one of resilience, empowerment, and security transformation at-scale.

Follow Juliet Okafor on her journey as she continues to break barriers, champion culture, and pave the way for a more inclusive and secure future in the world of cyber. Connect with her on:

LinkedIn - https://www.linkedin.com/in/julesmgmt

Website - https://www.revolutioncyber.com

CHAPTER 14

The Growth Mindset: Turning Challenges into Opportunities

By: Jarell Oshodi, Esq.

> *"You may encounter many defeats,*
> *but you must not be defeated. In fact, it may be*
> *necessary to encounter the defeats, so you can*
> *know who you are, what you can arise from, and*
> *how you can still come out of it"*
> *~Maya Angelou*

I can vividly recall that moment, etched in my memory as if it happened just yesterday. In a house full of family, with tears in her eyes, my mom told me that my dad died. At the tender age of six, I felt the weight of the world crashing down upon me. My protector, my best friend, my father, had been murdered in broad daylight. I was left with a void, an emptiness that seemed insurmountable. Who would provide for us, protect us, love and guide us? Who would impart life's invaluable lessons, the way only a father could? My questions hung in the air, unanswered.

Months later, my mom and I relocated to a new house in a different neighborhood, leaving the only home I could recall. There were no neighbors who looked like us, no kids playing outside, and no family within walking distance. My six-year-old life had been turned upside down and I had no choice but to adapt to this new normal.

The loss of my father brought with it a flood of emotions – grief, anger, sadness, confusion, and anxiety. In the midst of this storm, my paternal grandmother became my anchor. She shared heartwarming stories of my father, describing his great intellect and showing me the academic certificates he had earned, tucked away in her closet. She was so proud of her baby boy. I felt an innate responsibility to honor my father's memory by excelling academically. I was an only child, a straight-A gifted student, and now motivated to make sure my mom and grandmother were proud of me too. I thought I had a purpose.

Over time, my motivation remained unwavering. Regardless of the obstacles that came my way, I refused to be defeated by circumstances. I reminded myself that if I could endure the loss of my father, I could face any challenge that lay ahead. I was accepted into a prestigious public magnet high school in New Orleans, ranked among the top public high schools in the nation and best in the state of Louisiana. Upon graduation, I earned a full scholarship to Hampton University, then ranked as the number one Historically Black College & University by *U.S. News & World Report*. My journey continued as I graduated magna cum laude and earned another full scholarship, this time to Mercer University Law School. My family's pride knew no bounds. My grandmother would call me before she went to the senior center to find out my newest accomplishment to brag about me to her friends. Everything was going according to plan.

But life has always had a way of throwing me curveballs, and this time, it came in the form of a ruptured appendix during my first week of law school. To compound matters, the local doctor I encountered displayed blatant discrimination, depriving me of proper treatment for seven agonizing days. If it was not for my family's intervention, I would not be here today. Although I survived that ordeal, I had no choice but to withdraw from law school, spending weeks confined to bed rest. It was a setback, but I was not defeated. My spirit of resilience was strong as armor.

I had learned from various experiences that life's challenges are inevitable, no matter how hard we work or how meticulously we plan. These challenges tested my resilience and forced me to adapt, but I also knew that these challenges presented opportunities for growth and learning. Every time I faced an unexpected obstacle, I had a choice: I could either let it defeat me or rise to the occasion and find new ways to succeed. And each time, I chose the latter.

As I reflect on my life, I realize that being forced to withdraw from law school was a good thing. I had a one-year, non-academic break back home in New Orleans. For the first time in my life, as far back as I can remember I was not a student. I was able to be still and think about what I really wanted in life and what I felt my purpose was. While making others proud can be a great source of motivation, I realized that ultimately, I should be striving towards my own personal goals and desires. Relying solely on external validation was leading to burnout. Being self-motivated meant setting goals for myself and taking the necessary steps to achieve them, regardless of what others would think or say. I used the opportunity to find fulfillment in my own accomplishments and start working towards something that truly mattered to me.

Of course, it's important to have a support system of friends and family who encourage and believe in us, but at the end of the day, we should be motivated by our own passion and desire for success. By focusing on our personal goals and working hard to achieve them, we can find a sense of purpose and fulfillment that goes beyond just making others proud. I took advantage of the opportunity to spend time with family and friends. I worked as a congressional aide, legal assistant, and political campaign assistant. I even found my mother an off-market duplex to purchase. I returned to law school knowing I did not want to practice law and that was okay. I was still unsure of what I wanted to do, but knowing that I was open to the journey felt liberating. I graduated with honors only to pass the bar during a period of economic turmoil in 2010.

Although I was interested in the lucrative promise of the private sector, I'd learned that foresight was crucial in my personal life and career. I was no longer blindly doing what everyone thought I should do. When the economic recession hit and job stability became uncertain, I knew I had to be proactive. Instead of wallowing in despair, I researched the most stable career paths and realized that working as a federal government attorney was ideal for me. It would provide me with job security, a pension, opportunities for advancement, and the ability to make a positive impact on society. The work-life balance would also give me the flexibility to invest in real estate and maybe start my own business on the side.

When presented with the opportunity, I immediately accepted a job with the Department of Veterans Affairs adjudicating Veterans' claims for disability benefits in South Carolina. It was an incredible experience, and I felt that I was making a significant difference in people's lives. While there, the agency mandated that we go paperless, and I took the initiative to lead this massive effort. This experience working with cross-functional groups exposed me to the world of data governance, which would change the course of my career.

I discovered that as technology continued to advance and data became more important in decision-making processes, the demand for data governance careers was going to grow rapidly. I decided to pivot and take advantage of this growing career field, so I moved on to an opportunity with the National Institutes of Health in Maryland and later advanced to an opportunity with the Department of Justice in Washington, D.C. After five years of handling data governance matters, including the Freedom of Information Act and Privacy Act, I needed a new challenge. The job outlook reports for data privacy were positive, and I recognized the potential for growth in this field. I saw Europe was enacting the General Data Protection Regulation (GDPR) soon and decided I would take the CIPP-US certification exam. I knew this certification would help me demonstrate my knowledge and expertise in the privacy field, and it would give me a competitive advantage when applying for new jobs or seeking advancement.

But you know what they say, "If you want to make God laugh, show Him your plans." Life had a curveball for me yet again when my husband and I got pregnant, despite my doctor telling me the chances were low. Once our bundle of joy arrived, we realized we wanted to move closer to family, enjoy a lower cost of living, and move into a great school district to raise our child in. My husband was able to transfer his job to Georgia, and I left the Department of Justice to stay home with my miracle baby for a full year.

During my fifth month home with my son, I saw a Deputy Chief Privacy Officer (CPO) job announcement at the Centers for Disease Control and Prevention (CDC). I researched the role and my potential supervisor. I thought it was a great opportunity and cultural fit, but I knew in my heart I wanted to be home with my son for a full year, so I didn't apply, and the job announcement expired. A couple of months later, the GDPR became effective in May 2018 and although the U.S. had no federal privacy law on the horizon, I saw the increase of privacy job postings growing significantly all over the country. A month later, I studied for and earned the CIPP-US certification. As my son's first birthday approached, the CDC posted the Deputy CPO role again. I couldn't believe it. Was this my opportunity? The timing was perfect. Thankfully, my foresight paid off as I leveraged my skills and knowledge to become the Deputy Chief Privacy Officer of the CDC. This role allowed me to make a significant impact on the privacy policies and procedures of one of the most critical public health organizations in the world and my supervisor empowered me to insert myself where I saw fit. It was the first time in a long time that I felt comfortable showing up as my authentic self and feeling a sense of belonging in the workplace. That comfort was the icing on the cake and God's timing was perfect.

I'm thankful that I had the vision and ability to see beyond the present and plan for the future, ultimately leading me to a fulfilling and successful career in data privacy. By embracing the unknown and taking calculated risks, I was able to build a career in privacy that is the perfect fit for me and no one else. Not only do I feel empowered, I have the flexibility to partner with phenomenal organizations who sponsor my comprehensive global privacy training program called MIND URS®, reinforcing the notion that every employee plays a crucial role in becoming a privacy champion. This initiative emphasizes the importance of data protection in every role, cultivating a culture where privacy awareness is second nature. In today's interconnected world, breaches in personal data can have far-reaching consequences. Past trainees have provided testimonials emphasizing that the MIND URS® initiative is more than just a training program; it's a mindset shift.

As I reflect on my journey and the challenges I've overcome in my life, three constants have consistently helped me succeed: foresight, adaptability, and resilience.

These strengths are inextricably intertwined and have also been crucial in navigating my career in privacy.

1. **Foresight** or the ability to anticipate future developments, is a critical strength for success in any career, including data privacy. With the rapid pace of technological advancements and the constantly changing regulatory landscape, being able to anticipate and prepare for what's coming can make all the difference in staying ahead of the curve.

   In the field of data privacy, having foresight can mean proactively identifying potential privacy risks and vulnerabilities, and implementing safeguards to prevent data breaches or other privacy violations. It can also involve staying up-to-date on emerging privacy regulations and trends, such as the increasing focus on data transparency and data subject access rights. Foresight can enable privacy professionals to be proactive in their approach to data privacy, rather than simply reacting to incidents after they occur. In addition, having foresight can also help privacy professionals identify new opportunities for innovation and growth in the field of data privacy. By staying ahead of the curve and anticipating new developments, privacy professionals can position themselves as thought leaders, visionaries, and innovators in the industry and contribute to the development of new and effective privacy solutions.

2. **Adaptability** has been the cornerstone of success in my career. It is not just about being able to cope with the present, but about having the courage to face the future. It is about being able to anticipate and prepare for upcoming challenges and to identify and capitalize on new opportunities as they emerge. To be adaptable is to be open-minded, curious, and willing to learn. It requires us to step outside of our comfort zones and to challenge our assumptions, seeking out new perspectives and insights that can help us better navigate the complex and rapidly changing world of data.

At the heart of adaptability is a spirit of optimism. We have to embrace change as a natural part of life and see every challenge as an opportunity for growth and development. With adaptability as our guiding principle, we can thrive in the face of uncertainty, innovate in the midst of complexity, and succeed in a field that demands nothing less than our very best.

3. Finally, **Resilience**, is a critical trait that has helped me succeed in my personal and professional life, particularly in a dynamic and ever-evolving field like data privacy. The road to success is not always easy, and there have been times when I've faced setbacks and failures. However, I've learned to bounce back from these challenges, using them as opportunities to learn.

Being resilient in data privacy means having the mental and emotional fortitude to handle the stress and pressures that come with the job. It means being able to identify areas of improvement and continue pushing forward. In a field where data breaches, cyber-attacks, and legal violations are always looming, it's crucial to have a mindset that can withstand these challenges. Moreover, resiliency can help privacy professionals build trust with stakeholders, including clients, partners, and regulatory bodies. By demonstrating the ability to handle adversity with grace and persistence, privacy professionals can establish a reputation for dependability, consistency, and trustworthiness.

In combination, these three strengths - **Foresight**, **Adaptability**, and **Resilience** - have helped me go "far" in the constantly evolving world of data privacy. (See what I did there?) I've been able to leverage these strengths to overcome obstacles, seize opportunities, and thrive in my career. Through my experiences, I've learned that success in data privacy is not just about technical expertise or industry knowledge - it's about having the right mindset and a strong set of personal guiding principles to help you understand privacy compliance is not about laws, but about people. Once we change our mindset, we see that those who are able to anticipate future trends, quickly adapt to new challenges, and recover from setbacks are the ones who thrive. Looks like my dad taught me a few life lessons after all.

As you conclude this chapter, consider your personal growth journey. Cultivate a mindset that welcomes challenges, values persistence, and embraces change. Set specific goals for yourself, and view every experience as a chance to learn and evolve. Here are five steps to help you get started:

<u>Five Steps to Embrace Your Growth Mindset:</u>

1. **Cultivate Self-Awareness**: Start by becoming aware of your current mindset and how you respond to challenges. Recognize any fixed mindset tendencies and be open to change.

2. **Embrace Challenges**: Seek out and embrace challenges as opportunities for growth and learning. Step out of your comfort zone and take on tasks that push your boundaries.

3. **Learn from Setbacks**: View setbacks as valuable learning experiences. Analyze what went wrong, extract lessons, and use that knowledge to improve and grow.

4. **Value Effort and Process**: Shift your focus from outcomes to valuing effort and the process of learning. Understand that progress may not always be immediate, but consistent effort is crucial for growth.

5. **Persist and Celebrate**: Stay persistent in the face of obstacles, maintaining a growth-oriented approach. Celebrate your progress and achievements, no matter how small, as they contribute to your overall growth journey.

Remember, your mindset shapes your reality. So, take the first step today and embark on a transformative growth mindset journey that will lead you to new heights in every aspect of your life.

Jarell Oshodi, Esq.

Deputy Chief Privacy Officer | Federal Government

Jarell Oshodi is a licensed attorney, holding certifications as a Certified Information Privacy Professional and Certified Information Privacy Manager. Her career spans over 12 years, characterized by her instrumental contributions to government agencies in privacy and data governance capacities. Her roles include tenures at the Department of Veterans Affairs, National Institutes of Health, Department of Justice, and Centers for Disease Control and Prevention.

Beyond being a career public servant, Jarell is the Privacy Curriculum Director and board member of the Black Girls in Cyber, dedicated to empowering women in cyber and privacy through certifications and job opportunities. She lso provides keynote speaking, privacy training workshops, and on-demand e-learning modules globally. She has been named in the "100 Women in Cyber Project", "Four Leading Women in Privacy" by GRC World Forums, and "Black Privacy Stars." Her expertise has extended to influential roles as a thought leader for AfroTech, Digital Guardian, SecureWorld, and several other esteemed organizations.

Jarell's innovative approach is exemplified through her development of a privacy training initiative known as MIND URS®, designed to empower future leaders and foster digital responsibility. Her trainings have contributed to the development of thousands of privacy champions globally.

She holds a Bachelor of Science in Finance from Hampton University where she graduated magna cum laude and was honored as a 40 under 40 alumna. She also holds a Juris Doctorate from Mercer University.

Connect at:

LinkedIn - https://www.linkedin.com/in/jarellesq
Website - https://www.jarelloshodi.com

CHAPTER 15

When Dreams Become Reality "Navigating the Cyber Landscape from Practitioner to Entrepreneur"

By: Courtney H. Jackson

I went into the Navy right out of high school as an information systems technician (also referred to as an "IT"). This was the job that introduced me to the world of computers and technology-driven work. Up until that point, I didn't know a lot about technology outside of typing on a word processor and using dial-up to connect to the internet.

I remember Navy bootcamp as if it were yesterday. On the first day, there were people yelling in my face. They were called "Drill Instructors." I didn't know a single person amongst the eighty females in my bootcamp division.

I endured eight weeks of incredibly difficult training and often wanted to give up like several people had, but I didn't. The final test was called "Battle Stations." During that time, we had to stay awake for 24 hours straight, while completing a series of skills tests compiling everything we had learned up to that point. We did things like put out fires, pull heavily weighted objects through the water, and walk through gas chambers. One of the hardest parts was having to run from each battle station to the next while being extremely tired.

It was almost the end of Battle Stations. The final thing left to do was to run two miles to the finish line in a certain amount of time. I was excited, but exhausted at the same time. I was ready for it to end. I ran as hard and fast as I could. As I looked around people were passing me by, but I felt like I was running faster than I was. I made it to the finish line but had missed the mark by eleven seconds.

I was devastated! I had spent the past 24 hours enduring the hardest physical tasks I had ever faced. I made it across the finish line, but not in enough time. I literally fell to my knees and cried. It didn't matter that I had finished, I didn't make it in time.

My Drill Instructor told me and the others that didn't make it to grab some chow (food) and then go back to the barracks to rest up to attempt Battle Stations again–that night. The same night?!? How was that proper rest to endure another 24-hour race against time?

I messed over my food, honestly upset with myself that I missed it by eleven seconds. It may as well have been missed by an hour. Similar to a certification exam, no one wants to fail by a few points.

It took me a while to fall asleep, but I remember dreaming about my second attempt. In my dream, I passed Battle Stations! I was treated to a delicious meal, not the same galley food we ate everyday. I traded in my Recruit hat for a Navy hat, because I had made it.

Then the alarms sounded to wake me from my dream. It was Battle Stations time. I would not be defeated again!

I successfully completed all the tests and reached that final run again. I was shocked to have made it this far because I was even more exhausted considering I had just run Battle Stations the night before. But I was faced with that same obstacle that had defeated me – the final run.

I ran as hard as I could. My legs felt like they were on fire. My body ached like I had never imagined, and I had a hurt ankle. Despite those things, there was no way I was going to fail again. I crossed the finish line but this time, I made it! I had crossed the finish line before, but this time I made it before my time had run out!

I fell to my knees and cried again, but this time it was tears of joy.

Those of us who made it walked to the galley, and I remember thinking – "Great, all that and this same food." But it was the largest spread I had seen since I came to bootcamp. Delicious food and juices. We got to take our time eating versus our usual time-limited eating. Afterwards, we had a ceremony while they played the song "Proud to Be an American." Seems cliché, but when I tell you a song never hit as hard as that one did in that moment. I looked around the room filled with seaman recruits who had officially made it into the Navy. They swapped out our Recruit hats for Navy ones. This was all so familiar because it was my dream from the night before. Through perseverance, my dream had become a reality, and at that point, I felt I could tackle any obstacle that came my way.

From bootcamp I attended information system technician school in Great Lakes, Illinois. I learned a lot while there. I had no idea where I would be stationed after that. When I received my orders to Naples, Italy, I was excited and nervous. I had never left the country before. I didn't know anyone there, as none of my classmates got orders there. Yet I took the leap of faith into the unknown to try something new.

Being stationed in Italy turned out to be a great experience. I opened up, made some friends, and had a lot of fun. We were a two-hour drive from Rome, so we went there multiple times. I went to Milan, Pisa, Florence, and the beautiful Isles of Capri and Ischia. It wasn't all rainbows. I went through some trials and tribulations, but we'll save that story for another day.

After serving a few years of active-duty service in the Navy, I left with some IT experience specific to the military, which was outdated compared to the real world. After months of job searching, I landed a job at a help desk. I started off on the phones taking calls for customer issues such as password resets and connecting their computers to printers. My resolution and customer satisfaction rates were high, so I eventually worked my way up to a team lead position. I studied for and obtained my CompTIA A+ and Network+ certifications to learn more computers and networking.

From the help desk, I wanted to step it up a notch, so I secured a job as a desktop technician providing level-two support. This promotion got me off the phone and erforming hands-on work with customers. Most times it was user error, but sometimes there were legitimate technical issues that gave me the opportunity to learn new things. I did that for a couple years, then I took a job as a system administrator. In that role, I was responsible for creating user accounts, installing system patches, and maintaining the uptime which escalated my level of knowledge and hands-on experience.

My next role was at America Online (AOL) working in their Network Operations Center (NOC). Up to this point, I had experience working at a helpdesk, performing desktop support, and working as a system administrator. Working at the NOC exposed me to the networking side of IT. I enjoyed configuring network devices and troubleshooting network issues when outages were reported.

After I learned what I could in the NOC, my curiosity had me wondering about the security side of IT. That was one area I had not been exposed to yet, but security was not as popular then as it is now. After several months of rejected applications, I landed a job working in a Security Operations Center (SOC). I was familiar with NOCs, but I had no idea what SOCs were all about, which was very intriguing to me.

I was the only female on my team the entire time that I worked there, which was about a year. I was assigned to the overnight shift, which was not ideal, but I focused on the opportunity to get hands-on security experience. I am glad that I did. That was my first security job and in hindsight, the role was transformational for my career.

Leading up to this point (2008), I had self-studied for, and obtained, several certifications, specifically my CompTIA A+, Network+, and Microsoft Certified Systems Administrator (MCSA) certifications. While working the overnight shift, I studied for my CompTIA Security+ and ISC2 Certified Information Systems Security Professional (CISSP) certifications, while some others slept on the job (literally). I used that time to learn how to configure firewalls, Intrusion Detection Systems (IDSs), and Intrusion Prevention Systems (IPSs). This position really opened my eyes to the security and protection side of IT. Back then, it was simply referred to as "security," eventually it was called Information Assurance (IA) and now all the buzz is referred to as cyber.

After I gained hands-on security experience and my CISSP certification, I was promoted to a Security Control Assessor (SCA) position. Working as a SCA, I went to different customer sites to determine whether their systems and/or networks were up to par with the security standards that they were being assessed against. I worked as a SCA for a couple years while traveling across the country conducting assessments. We had internal checklists and Security Assessment Plans (SAPs) that we used, in addition to general resources such as DISA Security Technical Implementation Guides (STIGs) and Security Requirements Guides (SRGs) to assess each client's security posture. I ran vulnerability scans to check patch levels and known dependencies. I also conducted interviews with the staff to assess their security awareness, being that people are the weakest link in security. Building and executing the assessment plans for each customer engagement provided me with a well-rounded security experience and deepened my knowledge of the security implementations that should be in place.

From there I took a Security Engineer job, where I was assigned to specific applications while working alongside the software developers and management teams. It was my first exposure to implementing security within the software development life cycle (SDLC) and utilizing Agile methodologies. I attended scrums and sprint sessions with the development teams, ensuring security was accounted for along the way. Too many people make the mistake of addressing security after the fact versus embedding it from the beginning.

I was appointed as the company's first Information Systems Security Manager (ISSM), building their entire security program to encompass people, processes, and technology. This was a huge responsibility, but one that I embraced and worked tirelessly to ensure I fulfilled the role effectively.

I recall having meetings with external parties during that time. They would assume one of the males in the room was in charge of security until they were pointed my way, or I stepped in. Initially, I didn't feel comfortable speaking up, being that I was often the only woman in a room full of men.

It took time and confidence to demand the respect that I deserve.

I stayed in that role for a few years until I was ready to take things to the next level. My family and I relocated to another state so I could join a startup company working for a former boss. As the Lead Security Engineer, I had direct reports and more customer-facing interactions than before.

Since it was a startup company, I wore more than one hat from day to day. In addition to being a Lead Security Engineer, I was appointed as the Alternate Facility Security Officer (AFSO) and implemented the entire facility security program for that company. I did the self-inspections, created all corporate security policies, and went through the entire National Industrial Security Program Operating Manual (NISPOM) to ensure we were prepared for our first onsite audit (with me as the AFSO). I'm happy to share that we received zero findings on our first security audit, and we received extra credit for something that they called enhancements at the time, which was basically going above and beyond the minimum security standards.

Always go above and beyond in your career objectives and execution.

I was promoted to Cyber Program Manager, while working as a full-time security engineer and AFSO. When I took over the cyber program manager role that made me the highest-ranking security engineer in the company; there were over twenty employees, and I was the only female engineer. I successfully performed all three roles and became the go-to cyber Subject Matter Expert (SME) within our internal team and customers. My employer assured me that I was on track to become the next executive in the company. Imagine my surprise when a new male executive Chief Operating Officer (COO) was hired as my boss. I let it simmer for a while, but I had to speak up. I presented my case to the CEO demanding a higher salary and title based on my contributions to the company. I knew that if I didn't stand up for myself, no one else would.

Know your worth.

I negotiated directly with the CEO for my promotion to Chief Security Officer (CSO), which made me the only female executive in the company. While working as CSO, I was responsible for many areas of the business except contracts and business development, which in hindsight was intentionally withheld to keep me in a box. Even though I impacted organic financial growth based on my contract work, I was not given exposure to the traditional business development or formal contract management areas that involved bill rates. Despite everything I invested in helping the company grow, I did not feel appreciated or in a position for further professional growth.

The employees came to me when they had issues. I put out a lot of fires, and I was the highest-ranking security professional in the company. While I was making a good salary, my pay was not commensurate with the 50-60+ hour work weeks and contributions I was making to the company. It wasn't about the money. I started to wonder, "If I'm doing all this for someone else's company, why not do this for myself?"

That thought resounded in my mind for a while. I took some time to assess my career path and looked at all that I had accomplished to that point. There were no shortcuts. I served my country in the Navy. I worked my way up from a Help Desk operator to the Chief Security Officer for a multimillion-dollar government contract company reporting directly to the CEO. I had literally gone as far as I could in my corporate career, other than being a CEO. So, when I felt the time was right, I took the leap of faith into entrepreneurship.

I decided it was time to build my own dream instead of working so hard for someone else's.

My transition from practitioner to CEO did not happen overnight. I had to sit down and plan out my path. I made sure to save money while I was working as a CSO so that I could help support myself and my family during that time. I registered my business and started doing some part-time consulting work, outside of my day job (my employer was aware). I had to ensure it was something I truly wanted to do before walking away from my day job. Fortunately, I have a spouse who is very supportive of my business ambitions, so I did not have to do it alone. With that in mind, I dove headfirst into entrepreneurship after my husband and I decided to relocate from Maryland to Florida. It was the first move that wasn't driven by the military or one of our jobs. It was one of the first decisions I had made in a while that felt like I was putting my wants and desires first, versus doing something for someone else or planning based on some external factor.

It was a mindset shift.

I had to mentally prepare myself to shift from a steady paycheck to the unknown. When you work for a company, you know the frequency of your pay and the amount you'll be paid, especially if you're on salary. When you work for yourself, sometimes you don't know where that next payday is coming from or when it's coming, unless you have consistent work lined up.

Let's discuss some high-level steps.

With business, I always recommend obtaining legal advice, especially for anything concerning a non-compete agreement. If you start working on your business while you are currently employed, you want to ensure there aren't any clauses in your employment contract that could cause trouble for you. If you are clear to proceed, consider starting your business while you're employed so you continue to make money while establishing yourself as a new business owner.

After your legal advisor gives you the green light, it's time to register your business. There are a lot of companies that offer to do it for you, for a fee, but most states offer the option for you to register your business online. Once you register your business, secure your Employer ID Number (EIN) from irs.gov, which is free and easy to do.

As a next step, you should trademark your business name which you will need to consult your legal advisor to do. You may be thinking, "Why do I have to trademark my business name before I get my first customer?"

Aim high! Secure your business name from the beginning to prepare yourself for future success. I compare it to implementing security. It's best to do it from the start versus waiting until later, when it could be too late.

Now that you've taken care of those aspects, secure a website domain and social media usernames for your business to ensure consistency, even if you don't currently use all social media platforms.

When it's time to set up your website, there are many options. If you're creative and prefer to do it yourself, you can use free design templates online. Alternatively, there are many consultants available to build your website for a nominal fee. I recommend freelance sites such as fiverr.com and upwork.com to find a reasonably priced consultant. Be sure to check their reviews and portfolio so you can select someone with proven experience and a high client satisfaction rate.

Get a business checking account to keep your expenses and income separate. If you have a current bank, it's probably easier to go through them for a business checking account since you have an established relationship. When considering your banking options, find a checking account that doesn't charge you a monthly fee or a bunch of random service fees. Get a business credit card to use for all business expenses. I recommend using your business credit card to earn reward points, and then using your business checking account to pay it off each month to avoid accruing interest. Use software such as QuickBooks to track all business expenses.

Once you're set up for business, it's time to get some customers. The first thing you want to do is reach out to your current network. LinkedIn is a great platform to share business information to a large audience. Let the world know that you started your company and that you're available for XYZ type of work. Offer complimentary consultations, not only for the potential client to interview you, but for you to interview them. Early on, when I started my business, I jumped at most job opportunities because I was excited for the work. As I matured in business, I realized that every client isn't a good fit for me and vice versa. Utilize that initial complimentary consultation to assess mutual fit.

Select one or two core services to start out with. It can be tempting to list a bunch of services to cast a wide net and see what you catch but it can be confusing to a consumer. Think about trying out a new restaurant that you're excited about. Would you rather select from a one-page menu or a 10-page menu? Less options keep things simple, especially when you're just getting started.

This is not an all-encompassing guide to going from a practitioner to an entrepreneur but it's a great start. Writing this chapter reminded me of a business conference that I attended some years ago. There was a neon sign that said, "It Was All a Dream." Sometimes I remember that sign, and I have to pinch myself. I think back to conquering Battle Stations and dreaming about it before it happened.

I served my country, then started out at a helpdesk and worked my way up in corporate America from an administrator to an engineer, to a program manager, and eventually achieved Chief Security Officer status in corporate America.

After years of putting in tireless work to build someone else's dream, I am living my own.

I am the Founder and CEO of an award winning cyber consulting business. Competing in a male-dominated field is a driver for me to push harder and execute in excellence. If I had not pushed myself outside of my comfort zone to omplete Battle Stations and later take the leap of faith into entrepreneurship, I would not be where I am today.

Always go above and beyond in your career objectives and execution. Know your worth and that you are limitless. With hard work, dedication, and commitment, you can exceed your expectations and make your dreams a reality.

Courtney H. Jackson

CEO | Paragon Cyber Solutions

Courtney H. Jackson, MSISA, CISSP, CISM, CEH, CHFI is the award-winning Founder and CEO of Paragon Cyber Solutions, LLC, a woman, minority, veteran-owned cyber business based in Tampa, Florida. Mrs. Jackson is a 2023 Tampa Bay Business Journal Business Woman of the Year Honoree and the 2022 Global Cybersecurity Woman Entrepreneur of the Year. Her company, Paragon Cyber Solutions, is a 2023 GrowFL Top 50 Company to Watch Honoree, a 2023 Tampa Bay Chamber Small Business of the Year Finalist, and the 2022 & 2021 Tampa Bay Inno Tech Madness Champions.

Mrs. Jackson has more than 20 years of certified hands-on experience in Information Technology, encompassing both executive leadership and entrepreneurship. Through her work, she helps government agencies, tech startups, and commercial companies protect the integrity of their business operations through specialized cyber and risk management solutions.

In addition to a Master of Science degree in Information Security and Assurance and a Bachelor of Science degree in Business and IT Management, Mrs. Jackson also holds a number of professional industry certifications, including Certified Information Systems Security Professional (CISSP); Certified Information Security Manager (CISM); Certified Ethical Hacker (CEH); Certified Hacking Forensic Investigator (CHFI); Certified Penetration Tester (CPT), GIAC ISO-27000 accreditation, Microsoft Certified Technology Specialist (MCTS), CompTIA A+, Security+, and Network+.

Courtney's unique journey has positioned her to mentor women in male-dominated industries by helping them shatter the glass ceiling that stands in the way of their career advancement to executive leadership roles. In addition to programs that she has created to support the professional development of women, she also serves as the Vice President of the Women in Defense Greater Tampa Bay chapter, a member of the Military Cyber Professionals Association (MCPA), and a fellow of the Cybersecurity Forum Initiative (CSFI). She currently resides in Florida with her husband and children.

Connect at:

LinkedIn - https://www.linkedin.com/in/courtneyhjackson

Website - https://www.courtneyhjackson.com

Conclusion

This book is a love letter, tenderly crafted by a diverse group of women ranging from resilient immigrants to proud southern belles. The chapters etched within these pages extend a hand to anyone who has ever felt marginalized, disenfranchised, or devoid of hope, reassuring them that they are not alone, their battles are not fought in isolation, and their stories, too, hold the power to inspire and make a difference. The combination of narratives in the book forms a guiding light that illuminates the path for those navigating the challenging terrains of not just cyber, but any field where diversity and representation are the need of the hour.

Don't ever forget: You are more than enough.

You've got this and we are cheering you on!

This extraordinary assembly of authors, despite hailing from different backgrounds, cultures, and experiences, converge to share a common and powerful

message. They bring forth stories of perseverance and overcoming adversities, and recollections of triumph against the shadows cast by stereotypes, bias, and discrimination. Their narratives are rich with the diversity of their origins, the depth of their struggles, and the heights of their achievements.

We want to extend our deepest gratitude to you for choosing our book. We hope it serves as a significant guide, accompanying you through every stage of your career, from entry-level to the C-suite. It is more than a one-time read; it's a companion, designed to impart key insights on finding community, understanding your unique guidance system, continuing your education, and embracing your inner powerAs we turn the last page, we are not met with an ending, but rather a commencement. A beginning of a dialogue, a spark to ignite conversations, and a stepping stone towards a future where diversity is celebrated, inclusivity is the norm, and every voice, irrespective of its timbre, is heard and valued. "Securing Our Future" is not just a collection of stories; it is a call to action, a plea for unity, and a manifesto of hope.

**Disclaimer:** The views and opinions expressed by the authors in each chapter are solely their own and do not represent the perspectives of their employers or any affiliated organizations.

About Black Women in Cyber Collective

The Black Women in Cyber Collective (BWiCC) is a dynamic group of Black American women making an impact in cyber. This inspiring group of women are bringing their talents, skills and individual stories to the forefront as they make a collective effort to raise awareness regarding opportunities for Black women in cyber. Founded on a mission to empower Black women looking to make a career pivot into cyber or grow their careers, these women are looking to elevate the field of cyber and provide other Black women access, exposure, insight and sponsorship to change the face of cyber, privacy, online safety, data protection (e.g., encryption), or data governance.

In their highly anticipated and strongly supported new book "Securing Our Future: Embracing the Brilliance and Resilience Black Women in Cyber", the BWiCC narrates powerful stories of resilience, brilliance, transformation, and leadership laced with tips and tricks to starting, building, and advancing a career in cyber.

Made in the USA
Monee, IL
19 April 2024

57117968R00184